IMAGES
of England

WHEELS
AROUND
WESSEX

The Brit motorcar, of which there are no known suvivors. The Brit was produced in very small numbers, probably no more than three or four, by E.A. Chard and Company from 1904 to 1906. The second car out of their workshops is probably the one shown in this photograph, that was discovered recently by Tim Harding. The 8hp machine sported a varnished wood tonneau body and was allocated the Dorset mark FX 136 on 16 May 1904. The car was owned by William Saunders of 'Thornleigh' St Andrews Road, Bridport, who is believed to have been a director of W. Edwards & Son (rope, twine and fishing net manufacturers) of St Michael's Lane, Bridport. The only other Brits found in the Dorset County motor car registers are BF 100 (15 January 1904 to 14 June 1905), an 8hp tonneau for Edwin Chard; and FX 264 (30 April 1906 to 19 March 1910), a 12hp grey-coloured tonneau for William John Nantes (Nantes and Sanctuary, land and insurance agents) of 36 East Street, Bridport. In several modern, illustrated books of Dorset one can see a photograph of FX 482, the compilers of which believe it to be a Brit, but it is more likely that the car is the Aster 16/20hp model that was entered in the Dorset motor register on 9 October 1908, the number having been allocated to William Sidney Edwards (a former Mayor of Bridport).

IMAGES
of England

WHEELS
AROUND
WESSEX

Compiled by
Peter Daniels

TEMPUS

First published 2000
Copyright © Peter Daniels, 2000

Tempus Publishing Limited
The Mill, Brimscombe Port,
Stroud, Gloucestershire, GL5 2QG

ISBN 0 7524 1744 4

Typesetting and origination by
Tempus Publishing Limited
Printed in Great Britain by
Midway Clark Printing, Wiltshire

Peter Daniels, 'The Old Picture Detective', with a Moto-Sacoche engine-assisted pedal cycle of 1908 after having taken part in a Salisbury Hospital Carnival procession. The machine was restored many years ago by Charlie 'Crazy Bikes' Knight, who sadly passed away in May 1993.

Contents

Introduction

The discovery of a fascinating second-hand book in Bournemouth had such a profound effect on me it actually changed my life. The book, published in 1978, was by L. Fisher Barham who lived in Claremont Terrace, Falmouth. His album, part of the *Old Cornwall in Camera* series, illustrates the story of the area's road vehicles in old photographs – a remarkable collection of images depicting early motor cars, cycles and commercial vehicles. His research was probably centred on the motor vehicle taxation records at the Cornwall Record Office in Truro, which contains in-depth information about the vehicles, their owners and operators. Mr Barham successfully traced the descendants of many early car owners and their chauffeurs, and before long he had collected a surprising number of pictures. Thankfully, he had the enthusiasm, the desire and the time to prepare his research for publication, and there are now many transport and local history enthusiasts who are glad that he did. Sadly, although I never had the pleasure of meeting Mr L. Fisher Barham (he passed away in 1982), I will always be grateful to him for introducing me to such an interesting area of research. I cannot convey in words the excitement of finding a photograph of a rare, and sometimes unique vehicle, but I am sure that other collectors experience the same emotion.

My enthusiasm for road transport photography developed in parallel with my interest in the local history of Salisbury and its environs. Having compiled several books of photographs showing life in south Wiltshire in Victorian and Edwardian times, I was keen to produce an album of early road vehicles in the Wessex counties of Dorset, Hampshire, and Wiltshire. For almost twenty years I have gathered together an unbelievable number of photographs and facts concerning the private, public and commercial vehicles that have been used in this region over the past two centuries. Much of the information may have been lost forever had I not had the good fortune to discover it.

Our story begins in the late sixteenth century when long wagons, 'wains,' or 'machines,' as they were sometimes called, were introduced to Wessex. Used for transporting goods and passengers between towns, these wagons evolved into roomy vehicles, capable of carrying about twenty passengers, as well as goods. Running on broad, wooden-spoked wheels, they were heavy vehicles pulled by six, eight or more horses. An old English road-bill, dated 1774, records one of the wain services: 'The Rumsey Machine, through Winchester, hung on steel springs, begins flying on 3 April from London to Poole in one day.' Another advertisement for new stagecoach services appeared in *Mercurius Policus*, on 8 April 1658. It read: 'From the 26th day of April 1658 there will continue to go stagecoaches from the George Inn without Aldersgate, London, unto the several Cities and Towns for the rates and the times hereafter mentioned and declared – Every Monday, Wednesday and Friday to Salisbury in two days for XXs (20 shillings) and to Blandford and Dorchester in two days and a half for XXXs (30 shillings)'. This form of long-distance travel continued well into the twentieth century.

The introduction of self-propelled vehicles completed the last of three revolutions in transport that swept across Wessex, changing the lives of its people profoundly. The first began with the development of turnpike roads that ushered in the coaching era. The second, the introduction of the railways in the nineteenth century, brought the inevitable decline in road travel and transportation. Now, nearly two centuries later, road travel is very much back in vogue.

The earliest steam-powered vehicles to take to the lanes of Wessex were also manufactured in the region. A list of such companies would include Brown and May Limited, of Devizes,Wiltshire; E.S. Hindley & Sons, of Bourton, Dorset, The Liquid Fuel Engineering Company Limited, of East Cowes, Isle of Wight; W. Tasker & Sons Limited, of Andover; John I. Thornycroft & Company Limited and Wallis & Steevens Limited, of Basingstoke,

Hampshire. The government levied heavy tolls against the emerging road transport industry, effectively killing off large-scale development. In 1865 an Act of Parliament further restricted its progress by introducing a maximum speed limit for all mechanically propelled vehicles, of just four miles an hour in the country and half that in the towns. They were also required to have someone walk in front of them with a red flag to warn others of its approach. Furthermore, the vehicle could not be driven by less than three people. Thankfully, the regulations were reviewed in 1896, in the Locomotives on Highway Act, which permitted lighter vehicles to travel at twelve miles an hour. Another Act followed in 1903, which increased the maximum speed of vehicles weighing less than one-and-a-half tons to twenty miles an hour.

Another popular mode of transport, since the early 1900s was the bicycle. The earliest machines were known as hobby-horses or dandy-horses. Basically, they were bicycles without pedals or steering. Improvements to designs followed and by the 1860s there were several types of two, three and even four-wheeled vehicles. Virtually every town and village in Wessex would have had at least one business involved in selling and servicing bicycles. G Pooss, cycle agent, of the Triangle, Bournemouth, mentioned in the 1895 Western Gazette Almanac, is remembered as 'The King of the Scorchers'. He assembled a range of bicycles known as 'The Little Champion'.

Although motor vehicles were first manufactured in France and Germany, there were a few early models made and used in Wessex. One of the foremost motorists in the area was Frank Charles Carter, who purchased a Daimler from the Continent in February 1896. He was one of the first people in Wessex to commute regularly by road, travelling between his house in Bournemouth and his business in Wiltshire. He was the founder of Handel House Music Stores in Fisherton Street, Salisbury. His obituary in a local newspaper records that for a long time his car had been an object of much interest, as there were no others in the south of England, except in London. Ernest Hopkins, of Bradford on Avon, a professional photographer, would seem to have been the first person to build a practical car in Wessex. A photograph shows that his machine was a small, side-entry two-seater, with a front-mounted engine.

There were a number of other motor vehicle manufacturers in the region who seem to have vanished almost as quickly as they appeared: E.A. Chard and Company (Edwin Chard, proprietor) of St Andrews Road, Bridport, assembled Brit cars of which only about four seem to have been made. The old established coach-building firm of E. Channon and Sons made Channon cars in Dorchester. The Dorset vehicle registration records show that at least two of their motors took to the road: FX 196 (7 April 1905) was a blue-painted, 10hp tonneau for the personal use of Edward Channon of 6 High Street, Dorchester. FX 137 (number previously used on a Duryea tonneau) was a yellow-coloured landaulette for a physician named Telford Telford-Smith of 'Romansleigh', Wimborne.

In Wiltshire there was S. and E. Collett, of the Castle Street Garage in Salisbury, and Scout Motors Limited, of Bemerton. The Collett brothers made 'The Beaver', of which records for six cars and one van have been discovered. Issued with the Wiltshire registration mark AM 7357, the Beaver van was operated by Woodrow and Company (wholesale and furnishing ironmongers and brush manufacturers) of 5 Castle Street, Salisbury. It had chassis No.5008 and engine No.3176. The Scout motor company was founded by Joseph 'Percy' Dean, Albert Thomas Burden and William Burden in 1903. In Wessex, their production output up to 1921 was second only to Thornycroft. The Scout name was associated with agricultural and marine engines, motorcycles, cars, commercial vehicles (including ambulances and hearses) and charabancs. Thornycroft started manufacturing cars in 1903, but production had ceased by December 1913. The firm went on to establish itself as a well-respected maker of commercial vehicles. It was to be the last motor vehicle manufacturer in Wessex.

This book would be incomplete without highlighting the significant role played by the specialist motor vehicle manufacturers and operators used for public services. There were many manufacturers of these vehicles in Wessex, but Thornycroft was the only company constructing complete emergency, military and public conveyance vehicles. There have been many general commercial vehicle body builders who could turn out almost any kind of vehicle or body. There was Hampshire Car Bodies (HCB) of Totton; Hayden and Sons of Netherhampton, Wiltshire; H.W. Kiddle of the Old Tuckton Waterworks, Bournemouth; Lee Motor Works Limited, Bournemouth and J.H. Sparshatt and Sons Limited, of Hillsea, Portsmouth and Redbridge, Southhampton. Hampshire Fire Brigade Workshops, of Winchester built firefighting vehicles.

The years after the First World War saw a huge increase in the demand for charabancs and many ex-servicemen from Wessex set themselves up as bodybuilders or charabanc operators. In May 1922 Mark Briant, who ran White Heather Coaches in Bournemouth and a Mr Minns of Brighton, started an eight-day coach tour around Wessex, taking in Cornwall, Devon, Dorset, Hampshire, Somerset and Wiltshire. Their smart AEC and Daimler machines were all painted white and they ran on pneumatic tyres.

All those pioneering vehicles and their drivers have now disappeared over the horizon. They are gone, but not forgotten. Happy travelling!

IMPROVED FUNERAL GLASS CAR,
FROM
HAMMOND'S LIVERY STABLES AND TEMPERANCE HOTEL, BLANDFORD.
TELEGRAPH ADDRESS, "HAMMOND, BLANDFORD."

N.B.—Posting in all its Branches.

A Victorian glass-sided hearse. This advertisement appears in the 1890 edition of Kelly's Directory of Wiltshire and Dorset. The pair-horse carriage is typical of the glass-sided funeral cars that were very fashionable in the late nineteenth and early twentieth centuries. This particular one could be hired, along with numerous other kinds of horse-drawn conveyances, from Thomas Hammond of White Cliff Mill Street, Blandford.

One
Horse Power

A pony and trap in Bournemouth at the time of the First World War. This simple little vehicle, parked outside a house in East Cliff Gardens, is typical of the type of carriage used for general domestic duties at that time. It could be said that it was the equivalent of our present day small hatchback. This does not appear to be a casual photograph because two female members of the domestic staff (the housekeeper and a maid perhaps?) are immaculately dressed.

A north Wiltshire governess cart, after the First World War. The photograph, taken by George Woodfield, of 13 Bath Road, Swindon, shows three men and a boy enjoying a ride out on a bright, cold, day. This style of cart found universal appeal as a domestic runabout. It was ideal for transporting children to and from school. Access was by way of a single step and a door at the back of the body. It was well sprung to give a comfortable ride, and it was quiet, fast, and easy to handle.

Wiltshire day trippers ride out in a wagonette to Stonehenge at the turn of the twentieth century. The photograph is intriguing because modern-day restrictions prevent tourists from walking close to the stones, and one would almost certainly get arrested nowadays if caught driving a vehicle on the site. This dark-green, one-horse wagonette was hired out by Melville Whistler of the George Hotel in Amesbury. He ran a fleet of vehicles such as this throughout the early 1900s. His carriages had probably been assembled at C. Jerome's coachworks in Amesbury. By 1911 Mr Whistler was also hiring out motor cars.

Previous page, bottom: A one-horse phaeton at East Stour, around 1909. This style of carriage was one of the most popular types of horse-drawn vehicle to be used out of town. It was the MPV (multi-purpose vehicle) of its day. Ideal for transporting up to six adults, it could also be used as a dogcart or as a light load carrier. This particular vehicle is believed to have been constructed at Albert Chubb's coach building works in Station Road, Gillingham, Dorset. The photograph was produced and published by Phillips of East Stower (Stour).

A Royal Blue stagecoach in Bournemouth in 1912. This impressive four-in-hand coach was just one of a fleet of horse-drawn vehicles operated by Thomas Elliott. In 1880, at the age of 22, he founded his Job Master and Carriage Building business at The Royal Blue and Branksome Mews in Avenue Road, Bournemouth. The business thrived and in 1911 Elliotts Royal Blue purchased their first motor vehicles.

The Wiltshire High Sherriff's chariot in Salisbury, 1907. Here at St Ann Gate we can see an elegant looking carriage of the style known as a town chariot or a dress chariot. This particular one was the conveyance of Major Fitzroy Pleydell Goddard who was the last Lord of the Manor of Swindon. He passed away in 1927.

A single-horse Brougham on the Isle of Wight, in 1908. There were a relatively large number of horse-drawn carriages in use on the Isle of Wight in the early 1900s. A contemporary trade directory records that there were at least five coach and carriage builders operating in Newport alone. Lord Chancellor Brougham developed the design of this smart, neat town carriage in 1838. It was the forerunner of a multitude of four-wheeled closed carriages to be drawn by a single horse. Rout and Son, of 35 Carrisbrooke Road, Newport, built the one shown here.

A military pair-horse charabanc at Aldershot in July 1910. These are the men of the 2nd Lifeguards who were transported comfortably from Pirbright camp to Aldershot in this fourteen-seated conveyance. To name the vehicle correctly we should call it a wagonette, but in its day any horse-drawn carriage that was designed to carry twelve or more people was popularly known as a charabanc (the word comes from the French char-à-bancs. Carriage with benches). The charabanc proper had rows of seats fitted transversely, with each row having its own access point. The seats of a wagonette are arranged longitudinally, vis-à-vis fashion (face-to-face), as shown here.

A prize-winning bus at Wimborne railway station in 1905. Ingram Richards was proprietor of this smart station bus. Operating from the Crown Hotel in The Square, Wimborne, he ran regular services to meet the main-line trains arriving at the London and South Western Railway station and the Somerset and Dorset. A three-penny piece (3d) would cover the cost of the fare from the station to the Minster. This equipage has just won First Prize at a horse parade. The RSPCA organised annual carthorse parades in numerous towns across Wessex throughout the early 1900s. (The events held in Salisbury were among the grandest with classes for all kinds of commercial carriages.) In this particular picture there are a number of details to be read on the LSWR posters displayed under the canopy: Cheap Tickets Every Week-Day to Corfe Castle, Swanage and Weymouth; The Boat Train timetable; A special train for those wishing to attend a Blue Viennese Band concert. The stationmaster at the time was Sidney H. Smith.

Following page, bottom: 'The Winchester' mobile chapel at Alton, Hampshire, in around 1920. Operated by The Church Army, mobile units such as this were a common sight in the rural parts of Dorset, Hampshire and Wiltshire in Victorian and Edwardian times. The caravans were well designed for their purpose: There were steps at the front leading up to a covered platform, from which the minister would conduct his services. There was a letterbox and a knocker fitted to the double doors, which opened into the cabin. The interior was well illuminated by light cascading through the windows in the clerestory style roof. There were two beds, cupboards, a mirror and a water basin fitted. A light, portable foot operated organ would also be found inside. The photograph was taken by Henry Augustus Aylward, of 3 Market Street, Alton.

Military ambulances on Salisbury Plain, during the build up to the First World War. Here we can see a unit of the Royal Army Medical Corps taking part in a training exercise at Bulford, Wiltshire in 1913. The horse played a very important role in the British army, right up until the time of the Second World War.

A Dorset Constabulary dog-cart in the early 1900s. The photograph is thought to have been taken at Sherborne. This style of carriage was universally popular as a police vehicle at that time. In addition to transporting two people it could carry items of equipment and a dog. Unfortunately the name of the officer in the braided tunic has not been recorded. Do you know who he is? On the left stand PC 121 and PC 49, and on the right we can see PC 133 and PC 99. Accompanying the officer on the cart is PC 97. The original photograph, kindly provided by Dorset Police, has been badly damaged and only survives in two pieces. Jonathan Bingham has skilfully regenerated the image by pixel manipulation on a computer. The join, running from top left to bottom right, is now totally undetectable.

Following page, bottom: A horse-drawn hearse working in Southampton in 1908. We can see that a coffin containing the body of the late A.J. Carpenter is being moved from the back of the hearse and onto a hand-drawn bier. An area the size of Southampton and neighbourhood would have supported a large number of undertakers. In the 1907 edition of Kelly's Directory of Hampshire there are more than twenty listed. Not all of the firms would have owned a hearse; some of them would have leased a vehicle as and when required, a practice that is once again becoming commonplace because of the high cost of purchasing a new motor hearse.

A 50ft telescopic horsed fire escape in 1911, outside the Salisbury Council House (now the Guildhall) to commemorate the Coronation of King George V. The Salisbury Volunteer Fire Brigade was inaugurated twenty-seven years earlier in 1884. At the time of this photograph the Brigade comprized one captain (A.E. Rawlings), one second officer (W.E.M. George), two engineers, eighteen firemen and six auxiliary firemen. The wheeled appliances in use: one Steam Fire Engine (Shand Mason), one Horsed six-inch Manual Engine, one Horsed 50ft Telescopic Fire Escape (Built by Howard Harris & Son), one Horsed 50ft Telescopic Escape Ladder, one Horsed Hose Van and two Manual Hose Carts.

A donkey cart at Netley Marsh, Hampshire, 1908. The occupants would appear to be setting off for a wedding. Both the grey-haired old man and the boy are smartly dressed, with flowers in their buttonholes. There are no clues on the picture to aid identification, other than the sign-writing that can just be seen on the near-side shaft: J. Hindes, Netley Marsh. Little carts such as this were widely used by country smallholders.

Country carriers in the High Street, Downton in 1904. Nearest to the camera can be seen a common two-wheeled cart that was often the choice of vehicle used by tradesmen working in the building industry - bricklayers, carpenters, decorators, plumbers and such like. The four-wheeled wagon, however, was frequently employed by individuals and firms involved in general haulage or parcel carrying work. Coming into view in the background of the picture is the New Inn, of which Albert John Woodroffe was the licensee. Strong and Company, of Romsey provided their ales. The building attached to the inn functioned as a livery and bait stable at that time, offering good accommodation to commercial travellers, their horses and carts. The neighbouring thatched building was where Walter Durdle carried on his boot and shoemaking business for a number of years. His sign can be seen above the door.

Previous page, bottom: A two-wheeled water bowser at Bowerchalke, Wiltshire, 1911. Mr Penny can be seen here lifting water from a village stream with the aid of a hand pump. The vehicle appears to have been home-made (or should it be farm-made?), the barrel looks very much as if it had previously been used to hold alcohol of one kind or another.

A fishmonger's cart in Gillingham, before 1920. This is the two-wheeled cart used by William Kite to deliver fish to customers in and around Gillingham throughout the early years of the twentieth century. By 1939 Sidney Harold Kite had his name above the shop and the firm had progressed to delivering by motor van. The business was situated in the High Street. The fish was probably packed in cases in the back of the cart and insulated with wood-wool or straw.

A Portsmouth Corporation dustcart of the inter-war years. A heavy horse and a substantially constructed cart were requisite elements for this particular job. It was demanding work. The cart is very well designed for its purpose. The swan-necked shafts and small wheels permitted the use of a container with a large cubic capacity, but with the required low loading height. A screw mechanism has been fitted to the foremost chassis cross-member. This feature helped the dustman to discharge the load quickly and easily.

A Southampton market gardener's trolley in the early 1900s. This four-wheeled, single-horsed wagon was not built to carry an excessively heavy load. It seems to be perfect for the job in hand. The baskets of flowers have been marked with the letter W, suggesting perhaps that the cart was used by David, Charles or Walter Whitlock of Bursledon (market gardeners) or Emanuel Wills of Winchester Road, Southampton (nurseryman). The photograph was taken by James Eltringham of Portsmouth Road, Woolston.

One of many contractor's carts used in Wiltshire during the First World War. The firm of Wort and Way, based in Salisbury, were fortunate to have secured a government contract to construct military huts on Salisbury Plain from 1914 to 1915. It was a massive undertaking which they performed very effectively. The directors of the company were later to be congratulated for their work. This two-horsed vehicle, fleet No.19, is typical of the numerous agricultural wagons to be seen in the Wiltshire countryside during the late nineteenth and early twentieth centuries. This particular unit was used to carry hay from the railway stations to the army camps.

The Butcher. Here we can see Albert Baker and his wife with their 20cwt single-horsed van at Piddletrenthide in Dorset. This style of vehicle was very popular with bakers, confectioners, grocers, laundrymen and all types of retail stores. Two hinged and glazed doors were fitted at the rear of the body, above a hinged tailgate, that also functioned as a step, when hung in the down position. To facilitate the carriage of longer loads the tailgate could be supported in the horizontal position by chains. The thirty-inch wheels attached to the front forecarriage could be swivelled right under the bodywork, giving the vehicle good manoeuvrability. It could virtually be turned around in its own length. The photograph was taken before 1910.

Following page, bottom: No Candlestick Maker. The Fountain at Alderbury, Wiltshire, is the backdrop to this photograph of a single-horsed brewer's dray from Lamb's brewery, Frome. Drayman George Gater is seen here with his friend and four-legged companion, Bobby. The photograph was taken in 1913. Perhaps they had been delivering ales to the Green Dragon at Alderbury or the Three Crowns at Whaddon.

The Baker. This very smart turnout was one of a fleet of eight or nine similar vans operated by Nicholas Brothers of Salisbury. The quality of the coachbuilder's art is clear for all to see: the chocolate- coloured paint on this confectioner's van had been finished to a very high standard. Howard Harris & Sons of Winchester Street, Salisbury, built the vehicle around 1919. When this particular photograph was taken Douglas Oliver (driver/roundsman) and his boy were delivering bread to Miss H. Hussey of 58 The Close, in Salisbury.

A Wiltshire carrier departing from Devizes, in the early 1920s. Here we can see Harry Drake about to set off from Maryport Street on a journey to Salisbury, a distance of about twenty-five miles. The Three Crowns public house stands in the centre background. Harry farmed at Wick and on a fairly regular basis throughout the 1920s he loaded his cart with produce and carried it to the Tuesday market held in Salisbury. On a few occasions he may have been fortunate enough to find a client with goods to be carried to Devizes, in which case he would also return to base with a paid consignment.

Following page, bottom: A Hampshire pantechnicon from the early 1900s. This style of furniture removal van was generally made in three sizes, measuring 12, 15 or 18ft in length. On the shorter versions the front and rear wheels were often made of equal size and positioned below the floor line. On longer vans, however, such as the one shown here, larger rear wheels were fitted into semi-circular recesses (paddle boxes) that were provided in the body sides. An early colour photograph of a White two-horse pantechnicon has survived to give us a remarkably clear view of a pre-war furniture van. The forecarriage, shafts, wheels and under-floor well are all painted red, with dark brown coach-lining. The body pillars and roof boards are also red. The body sides are coloured dark brown and inset with a white band, outlined in red. The letters are painted in yellow, some of which have a light blue outline and others a light blue drop shadow. The White & Company lettering is light blue with a red outline. The firm was founded in 1871 and is now a very prominent name in the removals industry.

The Redlynch, Morgans Vale and Downton carrier, 1911. This was the van used by Frank Shergold of Woodfalls. Although it seems a good idea, it was unusual to see a carrier's cart with company advertisements painted on the side panels. The photograph records the occasion of the 1911 RSPCA carthorse parade, in which Mr Shergold was presented with a 'Special' prize for having the oldest carrier's horse at the event. The photograph was taken by F. Futcher & Son of Salisbury.

A United Dairies milk float some time after the Second World War. A large number of United Dairies vehicles were assembled in Westbury, Wiltshire from the 1920s onwards. The vehicles were used by United Dairies group companies all around Great Britain. The list would include London United Dairies, Wiltshire United Dairies, Alfred Slater of Birmingham, Cambrian United Dairies, Primrose Dairy (Cornwall) and South Eastern Farmers. It is worth noting the use of metal in the construction of the body of this milk float and the cast metal wheels fitted with pneumatic tyres. By the 1950s the era of the horse-drawn working vehicle was coming to an end.

Two
Cycles and Motorcycles

A meeting of the Salisbury Cycling and Athletic Club, August 1887. The members are pictured here in the shadow of Salisbury Cathedral. The club president, Mr William Pinkney (Director of the Wilts and Dorset Bank), stands just left of centre at the back of the group. He is wearing a bowler hat and some distinctive white side-whiskers. Several types of cycle can be seen here. On the left is a Dwarf front-driver, which appears to be sporting a 'Salisbury' lamp. Next in line is a tricycle and then a cross-framed rear-driver Safety bicycle. The two machines on the right are high-wheeled Ordinaries, popularly known as penny-farthings. This was before the era of the pneumatic tyre, so all these cycles are fitted with solid rubber tyres.

A Beaminster or Bridport boneshaker, in the late nineteenth century. This ancient-looking machine had developed from a two-wheeled conveyance, invented by Baron Karl von Drais of Karlsruhe in 1817. His machine was an instant success in London and it soon became popularly known as the hobbyhorse or dandy-horse. Propulsion was achieved by the rider simply pushing the ground with his feet. By 1861, however, pedal-driven models were being produced, like the one shown here in Dorset, around 1890. The original photograph carries the imprint of commercial photographer James Dare, who ran studios at Church Street, Beaminster and Barrack Road, Bridport. The name of the elderly cyclist has, unfortunately, not been recorded. The bicycle was already about twenty-five years old when this picture was taken.

A tricycle in Blandford before 1890. This spider-wheeled, sociable tricycle has rack and pinion front-wheel steering and lever brakes. With two experienced riders seated a good turn of speed can be achieved on machines such as this. Tom Nesbitt of 7 Market Place, Blandford, produced this carte-de-visite photograph.

The Embley Estate carpenter on his quadricyle, 1882. With more than sixty houses and farm buildings to be maintained on this south Hampshire estate, a reliable wheeled vehicle was an indispensable item of equipment for the estate carpenter, as some buildings were more than three miles from his workshop. This four-wheeled velocipede was rear-driven, with front wheel steering. A toolbox is fitted above the front axle.

Fashionable Southampton cyclists, before 1911. Bells, bonnets and baskets were the order of the day in Edwardian England. The two young female cyclists had just ridden through the Bar Gate. In the background can be seen two boater hatted males - one pushing a two-wheeled Safety, while the other vigorously peddles a tricycle into Above Bar.

A Piddletenthide carrier cycle at the time of the First World War. There were two basic styles of trade bicycle. The low gravity models incorporated a small front wheel that allowed a large basket frame and stand to be fitted. The other common design was a straight forward modification of the standard diamond-framed safety, such as the one shown here in Dorset. This particular machine was used by William Elsworth, who ran the Golden Grain Steam Bakery at Piddletrenthide for some years. The boy cycled around the local area making deliveries, while customers further afield were serviced by the firm's horse-drawn van.

Previous page, bottom: Dorset police bicycle forces at Poole Park, 9 October 1895. These diamond-framed bicycles appear to have been made by several firms, as there are numerous subtle differences in their styling. We can see that the fixed wheel model, shown fourth from left, has footrests attached to the front forks, to aid 'coasting'. The days of solid tyres had passed and all of these bicycles have cushioned tyres. Bells and moustaches were also very much in vogue. The original photograph bears the trademark of Job Pottle of Eastbrook, Wimborne.

A Lipton's box carrier cycle in Wiltshire, before 1920. This was the scene at Thomas Lipton's Silver Street outlet, in Salisbury, when the position of shop manager was changing. The original photograph carries a slightly sarcastic hand-written note: 'A bit of Lipton's Jam. The old and new Manager and Staff. More swank'. The box carrier was used to deliver tea and grocery orders to customers in and around the ancient chequered streets of the city. The photographic postcard was published by Horace 'Charlie' Messer, of Castle Street, Salisbury.

An unusual Wiltshire motor tricycle and trailer, built before 1903. This rare La Phebus-Aster motorcycle combination (AM 36) was registered to Samuel Augustus Smith of 1 Radnor Terrace, Queens Road, Salisbury. He was proprietor of the Handel House music store at 78 Fisherton Street, Salisbury. Manufactured in France in around 1900, his five-wheeled conveyance was not registered until new regulations were introduced in December 1903, which made vehicle registration compulsory. The AM letters were the first to be assigned to the County of Wiltshire. When the numbers 1-9999 had been allocated, four additional series of letters and numbers were issued: HR (from July 1919), MR (January 1924), MW (July 1927) and WV (August 1931).

An early Hampshire motorcyclist. The EL registration letters were assigned to the Borough of Bournemouth, in December 1903. The RU series followed in August 1924 and then LJ from July 1929. EL-51 was allocated to this 2½hp Royal Ruby machine, which was belt driven. This was the second issue of this particular mark, the vehicle was registered to William David Fford of 10 Lincoln Avenue, Bournemouth. Is this Mr Fford, with his pride and joy, outside the garden shed?

Here we can see Arthur Duncan Stratton (known as Bob to his friends) who took delivery of this 140lb Rex motorcycle (AM 398) on 16 April 1904. He lived at 'Giffords' in Melksham. Rex motorcycles were assembled at the Birmingham Motor Manufacturing Company Limited from March 1900 to June 1902, when the business was merged with Allard and Company of Coventry. The new concern was called the Rex Motor Manufacturing Company Limited. Production continued until 1911. This machine has a single-cylinder, side-valve engine and belt drive. A product ahead of its time, it was very reliable. During the first half of the twentieth century the Strattons gained a lot of experience with motor vehicles. The family was associated with the firm of Stratton, Sons and Mead, wholesale grocers and tea dealers, of High Street, Melksham. As well as the private cars of the directors and family members, the business fleet included Morris cars for the company representatives and Ford, Leyland, Scout and Thornycroft commercial vehicles for the transportation of goods.

Previous page, bottom: One of Tilley and Sons' motorcycles from Dorset. FX 319 was assigned to a 3½hp Rex motorcyce, for trade purposes, by M.H. Tilley and Sons, County Motor and Cycle Works, of St Andrew's Square and Victoria Street, Weymouth. In June 1908 the machine was sold to Charles Henry Right of 'Jerramine', Martinstown, Dorchester. Then, in October 1908, it was transferred to Harry Taylor of Hope Lodge, Great Western Road, Dorchester. Next it passed to Horace Greening of 32 Olga Road, Dorchester, who owned it from May 1911 to March 1912. Finally it found its way to Eric Winthrop Woodruff of HMS *Invincible*, in London.

Petrol and pedal power for Poole, in 1910. Here we can see a $2\frac{1}{2}$ hp Enfield Lightweight motorcycle, that was allocated the Dorset mark FX 700 on 7 October 1910. The machine was registered to F. & R. King & Co. of 198-200 High Street, Poole. It is believed that Mr King is the individual standing second from the left. The picture may have been taken at King's Cycle & Motor & Carriage Works, at Eastbrook House, Wimborne. We are not sure why the suited gentleman is holding an unfinished cycle wheel. Perhaps the picture was to be used commercially to show that the firm was involved in the manufacture of spoked wheels. It can be seen that the carrier bicycle had been sign-written for F. & W Palmer, purveyors, of Poole.

'TR 327', a much travelled Matchless in the 1920s. F.A. Hendy & Co. Limited registered this chain-driven motorcycle on 12 May 1925; their offices were at 68 Above Bar, Southampton. Four days later they sold the machine to August Vincent Carbini of 2 South View, Winchester. Records show that the L4 model Matchless had frame No.3701 and engine No.L3012. Mr Carbini appears to have moved around quite a lot; several addresses are shown on the logbook, including Harrogate in Yorkshire. On 1 July 1927 the ownership changed to Henry William Pearce, of the Hampshire Constabulary, West Hill, Winchester, and then, on 20 July 1928 the motorcycle was transferred to Arthur Charles Pearce of the Broadmoor Asylum in Crowthorne, Berkshire. We believe that the machine was eventually broken up. This picture of Mr Carbini was taken by Henry George Osborne of East Street, Alresford.

Previous page, bottom: A Bournemouth boy racer of the 1920s? Here we can see EL 4912, a 7-9hp Indian V-twin model that first took to the road in April 1920. The registered keepers were Ivan and Fred Horne of 81A Walpole Road, Boscombe, Hampshire. The rider is well equipped to drive this smart turnout, which features disc wheel attachments and sports handlebars.

A Dunelt on the Isle of Wight. Unfortunately, the registration records appear to have been lost, so no detailed information is available for this chain-driven motorcycle or its owner. Do you recognise him? The first DL mark was issued in December 1903 and the series continued until 1935 when DL 9999 was allocated. DL 4728 was probably issued in 1926. The Dunelt motorcycles were made by Dunford and Eliott (Sheffield) Limited at their works in Smethick, Birmingham. The picture appears to have been taken near Blew's pleasure boat booking office on the esplanade at Shanklin.

A family photo opportunity at Eastleigh in the thirties. This sturdy-looking Rudge Special was supplied by Alec Bennett, a motorcycle expert, of Portswood Road, Southampton. From 27 January 1928 its first registered keeper was John Compton of 9 Mount View, Eastleigh. The 5hp machine had frame No.26687 and engine No.47706. In October 1937 it found a new owner in London, one Richard Copsey of Muswell Hill.

A winner from Warminster in the thirties. Leslie Hill is pictured here with the 346cc OHV Federation motorcycle, on which he won many awards as a private entrant in trials organized by the MCC and other clubs in the Salisbury District. Living at 32 Market Place, Warminster at the time, he was allocated the Wiltshire mark MW 7692 in July 1930. Federation motorcycles were marketed by the Co-operative Wholesale Society of King's Road, Birmingham. The one pictured here is a $2\frac{1}{2}$ hp model 10Y with frame No.2630 and engine No. W 56110.

A Léon Bollée voiturette at Stonehenge, in the late nineteenth century. When production of this tandem tri-car commenced at Le Mans in 1895 it was faster than any other petrol engined vehicle on the road. Its 650cc single-cylinder, air-cooled engine was rated at 3hp. The rights to the design were sold to Darracq in 1901. The owner of this particular machine is believed to have come from Pewsey. No records of the vehicle have survived.

A Humber cyclecar in Hampshire, before 1910. This Bournemouth registered conveyance (EL 292) took to the road in May 1905. William Herbert Daniel was the first owner; he lived at 184 Holdenhurst Road, Bournemouth. In February 1907 he sold the tri-car to James Hampton of 'Ashdene', Richmond Gardens at Portswood, Southampton, with whom it remained for two years. From 6 April 1909 the new keeper was George Harold Gendall, the Headmaster of Brockenhurst Elementary School. He lived in the School House. Humber was just one of many British firms that made three-wheeled cyclecars. The early machines, such as the one shown here, featured handlebar steering and a sprung saddle. Later models would have a steering wheel fitted, and a padded, framed seat for the driver. The Humber had an excellent reputation.

Following page: An LMC military combination at Tidworth barracks at the time of the First World War. This 3½hp LMC model was manufactured at the Clyde Works of the Lloyd Motor Engineering Company Limited (7 Freeman Street, Birmingham) in 1914. Allocated the Southampton registration mark CR 2656, it carried frame No.1636 and engine No.2233. On 3 June 1921 the vehicle was acquired by Lionel Archibald Wright of 4 Gloucester View, Green Road, Southsea. At the end of May 1922, having used it for just twelve months, he sold the combination to Edgar George Coward of 57 Abingdon Road, Southsea. The original photograph appears to have been taken by Frederick Wright, a commercial photographer, of 73A High Street, Andover.

Rowland and Sons' motor cycle repair depot at Salisbury, in 1903. William Rowland founded his cycle engineering business here at 13 Caste Street, Salisbury in 1899. Here some mechanical adjustments were being made to two motor vehicles. On the left we can see a Scout $2\frac{1}{2}$ hp motor-bicycle, from the works of Dean and Burden Brothers in the Friary, Salisbury. When vehicle registration became compulsory in January 1904 this machine was allocated the Wiltshire mark AM 269. Its owner was Edwin Scammell of 5 Nelson Road, Salisbury. On the right is a rear-engined quadricar, for which no information could be found.

A Roper-engined rarity in Swindon, before the First World War. J. Roper of Birmingham Road, Wolverhampton was principally a cycle component and fitting manufacturer, but a small number of complete machines was also assembled. This 4hp model (AM 2371), with its wicker sidecar attachment, was registered to Richard William Jones of 26 Commercial Road, Swindon, in 1912. The machine appears to have been unreliable, because it changed hands quite frequently. Its last days were spent in London with an owner named Noah Welch of 356A Barking Road, West Ham.

AM 4736, well travelled around Wessex. This well presented Royal Enfield motorcycle and sidecar combination was first seen around the roads of south Wiltshire in April 1915 with its owner, Joshua William Lewis, of 46 Belle Vue Road, Salisbury. Three years later the machine passed to Frederick Miller who lived a short distance away in York Road. He was the owner when this photograph was taken. On the back of the original print can be seen a message from his wife or sister, Georgina Miller, who was sending the reader her Best Wishes. Perhaps Georgina is one of the smartly dressed women shown here? In May 1919 the vehicle found a new owner in the West County at Plymouth. After just a few weeks Philip John Symons of Pentyre Terrace sold the conveyance to Harry Hamilton Evans, an officer on HMS *Thunderer* at Portland, Dorset. Then in 1927, after passing through several other hands in the Weymouth area, the 6hp Royal Enfield ended its days back in Wiltshire with William Douglas of Cleave House, East Knoyle.

Previous page, bottom: A Bradbury and sidecar from Winchester, before the First World War. This 4hp machine was manufactured in Oldham, Lancashire by Bradbury and Company Limited, of Wellington Street. In April 1911 it was driven away by its first owner – George Lake of 29 The Square, Winchester. Two years later he sold it to George Honeyborne, who lived at 'Denehurst' in Winchester Road, Bassett (near Southampton). In January 1915, the motorcycle and wickerwork sidecar combination passed into the hands of Frank Barber of 'Tarrants', West Wellow. He was an accomplished photographer and the first newsagent in the village.

A panther on the prowl in Dorset? It is rather unfortunate that many of the early Hampshire motor taxation and registration records have been mislaid or lost. It is very difficult therefore to discover very much about the ownership and movement of certain vehicles registered in the AA, CG and HO series. The records for this particular Panther motorcycle and sidecar (AA 8919) cannot be found. The photograph was almost certainly taken at the RAF camp at Blandford on one of the many visits by Frederick Mitchell, a commercial photographer, based at 1 Exeter Road, Poole.

Oh you two - who are you? This tantalizing photograph of a Hampshire motorcycle and sidecar would seem to be destined to withhold its secrets. Despite having made numerous enquiries about the vehicle and its desirable numberplate, the author has turned up very little information. All that is known about the Hampshire mark OU 2 is that it was allocated to a Riley motor vehicle in the ownership of a Captain Martineau of Abbotts Ann, near Andover in October 1928.

Two, three and four-wheelers from the thirties. In the foreground of the picture we can see a Hampshire registered BSA motorcycle combination (HO 922), which stands alongside a four-wheeled cycle-car, origin unknown. Parked at the back of the group, with its hood up, is a Morgan three-wheeler (HO 3890) of 1920. We do not recognize the location- does it look familiar to you?

The funeral of a Hampshire motorcyclist, before the Second World War. The cortege comprises a Triumph motorcycle combination, carrying floral tributes, followed by an Austin hearse and three Austin mourning limousines. The motorcycle shown to the left displays the Hampshire registration mark OU 5571. The funeral of A. Frankham is believed to have taken place in or around Bishops Waltham. Unfortunately, no other details are known.

Three
Edwardian Motorcars

The first motor car to have been registered in Portsmouth, 1903. A complete set of records does not exist for this conveyance, but it would appear to be a 12hp chain-driven phaeton manufactured by Panhard et Levassor of Paris, in around 1900. The car was registered to the Portsmouth Borough Engineer and Surveyor. The registration mark BK 1 has been re-issued and transferred on numerous occasions since its first appearance in December 1903. Many years later Portsmouth Borough Council acquired the number for use on the mayoral car.

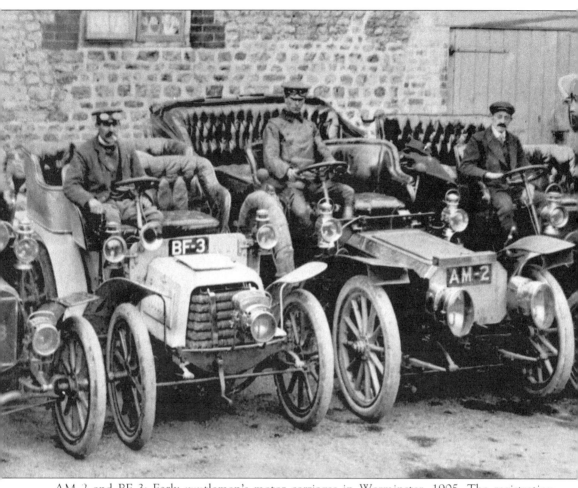

AM 2 and BF 3: Early gentlemen's motor carriages in Warminster, 1905. The registration letters AM were allocated for use on motor vehicles in the county of Wiltshire. On 11 December 1903 the mark AM 1 was allocated to the County Surveyor. A few days later AM 2 was assigned to John Benett-Stanford of Pyt House, Tisbury. The recipient vehicle was an 18/22hp Peugeot, with a green painted tonneau body and brown leather upholstery. Its wheels were painted yellow. Fourteen months later Mr Benett-Stanford bought a new car and the AM 2 plate was transferred to a Peugeot with a 25hp engine and a side-entry body. The car can be seen parked alongside a 10hp Panhard rear-entry tonneau, that carried the Dorset mark BF 3. This car was owned by Sir Randolph Littlehales Baker Bart JP, of 'Ranston', Iwerne Courtney, near Blandford. Originally painted cream, with red coach lining (as shown), the body was later repainted in a dark shade of green. The implications of the letters BF were the cause of much embarrassment to early motorists in Dorset, so on 27 December 1904 a government department allocated the replacement mark FX. Of the original 162 numbers issued, more than eighty motorists decided to retain their BF plates. Sir Randolph was one of them.

AA 4: A doctor's car, often to be seen around Lymington. This 12hp Richard-Brazier side-entry car is the second vehicle to have been allocated this early Hampshire mark. Its owner was Alexander Drimmie Pithie, who was a physician, surgeon, and the Medical Officer and Public Vaccinator for the district of Lymington, Hordle and Milford. His address was 1 High Street, Lymington. By 1915 the car had passed to Joseph Ross of 12 Orchard Place, Southampton. The photograph was taken by Frederick James Arnott of 120 High Street, Lymington, in 1906.

AM 6: An amusing Sunbeam-Mabley car from Melksham, June 1906. This odd-looking machine, designed by Mr Mabberley-Smith, was produced by the Sunbeam Company from 1901 to 1904. The wheels are placed in a diamond formation, with the front and rear wheels staggered on each side of the centre line. Powered by a $2\frac{1}{2}$hp De Dion engine, the car had tiller steering. The photograph, taken in Bank Street, Melksham, shows (from left to right) Messrs J. Fisher, E.J. Hughes and A.M. Smith.

EL 8: The first Benz motor car to be registered in Bournemouth, 1903. This 1½hp motor carriage was manufactured in 1898, but was not allocated a registered mark until the introduction of the Motor Car Act in December 1903. Its first owner is believed to have been The Imperial Motor Works of 7 Holdenhurst Road, Bournemouth. The car was dark green in colour.

BF 27: one of Lord Wimborne's quality motor cars from before 1904. Records show that The Rt Hon Ivor Bertie, the Lord Wimborne of Canford Manor, registered four cars on 18 December 1903. BF 27 was allocated to this turn-of-the-century 12hp Panhard rear-entry tonneau, which was painted yellow, with black coach-lining on the wheels. BF 28 was attached to an electric Brougham and BF 29 to a Daimler limousine. The BF 30 mark was issued to Lady Wimborne for use on her De Dietrich side-entry car. On 4 April 1909 Lord Wimborne sold the Panhard to William Moore Bell of Heather Grange, Ringwood, who does not seem to have been too concerned about the connotations of the BF registration letters, which embarrassed and upset so many other early motorists in Dorset.

Previous page, bottom: DL 20: An early Dennis model from the Isle of Wight. This handsome side-entry, 'Roi-de-Belge' bodied car is the second machine to have been adorned with the desirable mark DL 20. A photograph also survives of the first car – a 12hp Wolseley rear-entry tonneau which was the pride and joy of Doctor John Livesey JP of Belgrave House, Ventnor. It is not known if the Doctor was also the proprietor of the car shown here.

CR 52: A Southampton Traveller from the dawn of the twentieth century. The only known record of this particular Southampton registration mark dates from 16 July 1907. Unfortunately no details are given about the vehicle kept at that time by Amos Thomas of Ashton Villas, Guest Road, Bishopstoke. The car shown here, with the CR 52 mark, is an Alldays Traveller, a wheel-steered cycle-car made by Alldays and Onions Pneumatic Engineering Company Limited of Birmingham. It is powered by a 4hp De Dion single-cylinder engine, located under the driver's seat.

Following page, bottom: AA 142: A tiny Napoleon two-seater in Fordingbridge, Hampshire, before 1910. This is a very rare car of which very little is known. It was imported from France in around 1902 and found a home with Robert James Neave of 'Inglenook', Fordingbridge. Powered by a single-cylinder, water-cooled, 6hp De Dion engine, the car has a three-speed gearbox and shaft drive. Having been used by the Neave family for some time the little two-seater was acquired by Air Vice Marshall Sir Alec Coryton of Langton Matravers, Dorset. Eventually it passed to J.M. Clarke of south west London. The car is still in existence.

FX 84: a Humber two-plus-two from the Isle of Wight, 1910. The Dorset mark BF 84 was first allocated to a Beaufort phaeton, owned by Sam Long of Blandford, but in December 1904 he exchanged it for the less controversial mark FX 84. When he sold the car six years later, the number was re-issued for use on this bright blue Humber. It was a 12hp two-seater, with dickey seat. By this time Mr Long was residing at Shide House, at Newport on the Isle of Wight. The car was far from home when this picture was taken- the original print carries the trademark of Bell and Sons of Shepton Mallet.

AM 174: A mystery motor from Melksham, before 1904? The only record that survives for this particular Wiltshire mark refers to a red coloured Renault, fitted with phaeton-style bodywork by the Iveagh company. The general appearance of the vehicle would suggest that it was manufactured before 1900. On 6 January 1904, to comply with the Motor Car Act of 1903, the car was registered to Tilkes Smith of Avon House, Melksham. Eight years later it found its way into the hands of a new owner in Scotland. He was one William McCoss of 23 Windmill Brae, Aberdeen. Although several experienced automobile historians have studied the photograph neither of them is prepared to say whether or not it portrays an early Renault motor car. The car is certainly very unusual.

Following page, bottom: AA 222: A Thornycroft, built in Basingstoke, driven in Dorset. This wire-wheeled, 18hp Thornycroft is the second car to have carried the Hampshire mark AA 222. From January 1911 to February 1915 it was owned by Henry Welch Thornton of Sherborne St John, near Basingstoke. A side-entry model, it has two windscreens fitted – one at the front and one at the rear. A fishing-rod basket can be seen lying across the rear mudguard. The car is fitted with acetylene and electric powered lamps.

EL 192: A green Gladiator at Bournemouth in the summer of 1906. Here we can see members of the Quertier family in front of their house, Holme Dene, in McKinley Road, Bournemouth. Their carriage is a 12hp Gladiator rear-entry tonneau that was registered on 9 May 1904 (its first owner was Harold Simmons, a surgeon, who lived not far away in Christchurch Road). Having acquired the car in May 1905 Josiah Quertier appears to have kept it for just twelve months, because on 25 May 1906 it was transferred to Thomas Percy Smith of Nelson, Lancashire, who is believed to have been a scrap metal dealer. The Quertiers, incidentally, were fruit growers at Ashford Vineries, near Fordingbridge.

AM 540 and AM 903: Quality cars at the Bapton Manor motorhouse in 1912. The green-painted landaulette shown to the left was the second of three 20hp Spyker cars to have displayed the Wiltshire mark AM 540. The first car was a side-entry, 'long chassis' model, registered to Joseph Deane Willis (born 23 January 1859), farmer and landowner of Bapton Manor, near Codford, on 19 October 1904. The mark was transferred to the landaulette in January 1907 and stayed with the car until a stone-coloured Spyker cabriolet replaced it on 27 December 1915. The second car pictured here (AM 903) is a 40hp Mercedes 'Roi-de-Belge' tourer that had been painted in a dark shade of green with red wheels. Mr Willis ordered this particular car in June 1910 to replace a two-year-old 40hp De-Dietrich side-entrance model that had originally carried the AM 903 number-plates.

FX 620: A Singer five-seater from Weymouth, May 1910. Daniel Guy can be seen here in the driving seat of the green-coloured hackney carriage he purchased in April 1910. He lived at 5 Johnston Row, Weymouth. Three years later the car was sold to Ernest Edmund Dalton of Cerne Abbas and by July 1920, having passed through the hands of several owners, the 12/14hp side-entry motor car was in the possession of Joseph Cook of Yeovil. The photograph was produced by Walter Thomas Dovey (photographer and stationer) of 13 St Thomas Street, Weymouth.

EL 759: A Motobloc two-plus-two in Bournemouth, before 1914. Very few Motobloc vehicles have been seen on the roads of Wessex at any time. This rare, 14/16hp general purpose model was purchased by Neil MacGillycuddy of 'Pendennis', 7 Derby Road, Bournemouth in October 1909. Goods could be carried on the rear platform, beneath which a folding dickey seat was to be found. In the bottom left corner of the picture we can see the imprint of photographer Frank Grimmett of 10 Royal Arcade, Boscombe.

FX 907: A watchmaker's Model T Ford from Dorchester, before 1918. This black painted 20hp four-seater was first registered to M.H. Tilley & Sons (gold and silversmiths, watchmakers, jewellers and opticians) of South Street, Dorchester on 3 March 1911. The car appears to have been quite new when this photograph was taken. Note the uniformed chauffeur and the Stepney spare wheel. Among later owners of the car were Thomas Maggison of High West Street, Dorchester and Tilleys (motor engineers) of Victoria Street, Weymouth.

AM 1161: A dark blue Wolseley landaulette in Swindon, 1911. This is the second car to have been allocated the Wiltshire mark AM 1161. Both vehicles were owned by Frederick George Wright of 'Toynton', 52 Bath Road, Swindon. This elegant 20/28hp model took to the road for the first time in August 1910. It had primrose-coloured wheels with white tyres, black leather upholstery and brass fittings. Mr Wright, whose family arms were painted on the passenger compartment doors, was a very well known individual in his locality. Having worked for the Great Western Railway Company since 1892, he was appointed to the position of Swindon Works Manager in 1901. The following year he was elected Mayor of Swindon. By August 1919 this very smart motor car was owned by an Alex Richardson in London.

Previous page, bottom: BK 922: A Portsmouth hackney carriage, at the time of the First World War. A complete set of records for this taxi-cab has not survived, but we believe that it is just one of a fleet of cars based at the Colonnade Garage in Portsmouth. Stanley Simmons was the proprietor. This particular motor-cab would seem to be a Unic that was painted royal blue. The landaulette style bodywork and the white tyres gave it a very smart appearance. Looking through the windscreen one can just see the 'For Hire' flag attached to the taxi-meter. In addition to the Unic Mr Simmons ran several 12/14hp Humbers, including a landaulette (BK 1965) and a side-entry model with cape cart hood (BK 5572). The photograph was published by King & Co., of 38-40 St James's Road, Southsea.

DL 1170: A Scout hackney carriage on the Isle of Wight in the 1920s. Manufactured in 1912, this semi-closed-drive landaulette is typical of the medium sized cars being produced by the Scout Motor Company at Bemerton in Salisbury, before the First World War. Their first car was assembled in 1905 to take part in the Tourist Trophy race, held at Douglas on the Isle of Man in September of that year. It was one of only nine cars to cross the finishing line. Production of Scout cars and commercial vehicles continued until 1921. A photograph of a Scout Ambulance can be seen on page 115. The crimson-coloured, 24hp motor-cab shown here was believed to have been employed for a number of years by E.H. Crinage of 'Roslyn', Hamboro Road, Ventnor.

Following page, bottom: EL 1346: Miss Handsley's little Renault, at Bournemouth in 1913. This tiny Renault 8hp two-seater was the first car to have been driven by Miss Florence Adeline Handsley. She lived at West House, 30 Portarlington Road, Bournemouth West. The car was painted grey, with fine blue lines picking out the wheels, wings and bonnet. While on the subject of bonnets, take a glimpse at Miss Handsley's outfit – she is appropriately dressed for a drive in her motor car.

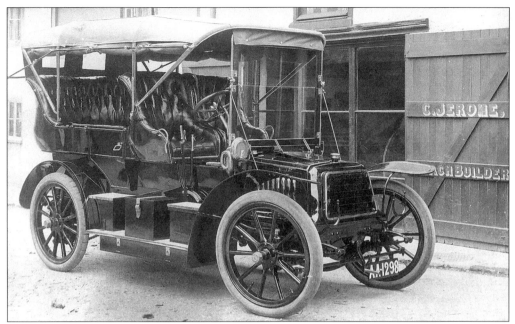

AA 1298: A highly polished side-entry Panhard, at Jerome's Andover Coachworks, 1912, built for Alfred Head of Buryhill House, Anna Valley, near Andover. The car is a side-entry model, fitted with a cape cart hood. The body was later transferred to a chassis made by the Scout Motor Company in Salisbury. Mr Head was the founder of the Anna Valley Motor Company, which went on to open branches in, among other places, Salisbury and Winchester. His chauffeur at the time of this picture was Alford Roe, who also did fairly well in the motor business. He started a haulage company based at 76 Charlton Road, Andover.

AM 2072: Revd Lenthall Greville Dickenson's Metalurgique Motor at Downton, Wiltshire, during the First World War. Registered in Witshire on 8 August 1911, he purchased the 20hp, torpedo-bodied car in 1915. Revd Dickenson had been the vicar of St Lawrence's church since 1910. Pictured here with the French grey-coloured car is Reg Moore, the chauffeur, who lived at Church Hatch in Downton. In 1919 the car was sold to James Walgrave Collier of 56 Princess Road, Leicester.

AA 3511: A Sunbeam landaulette from Bitterne Park, Southampton, 1913. This dark green machine first took to the road on April Fools Day, 1911. It was originally owned by John L. Bond of 'Harefield', Bitterne. In June 1913, following the death of Mr Bond, the car was acquired by Louise Fanny Thomas, who owned it until 1914.

Four
Charabancs, Buses and Coaches

One of the first motor omnibuses to be seen on the Isle of Wight, 1904. Carrying the Isle of Wight registration mark DL 78, this 30hp Milnes-Daimler double-deck omnibus is pictured here in the High Street at Ryde. One of the unusual features of the machine was the wicker basket fitted on the roof, above the driver's compartment. Passengers could place their luggage in the container when riding on the upper deck. It is thought that the Isle of Wight Express Motor Syndicate Limited was the operator of the vehicle. Milnes-Daimler motor omnibuses such as this were a popular choice of railway companies. The Great Western Railway Company, in particular, ran many of them around the Wessex region.

The new Lymington motor omnibus in 1905. Seen here passing William Elgar's shop in Lymington High Street is an MMC (Motor Manufacturing Company of Coventry) covered charabanc, returning to the town after a round trip to Milford-on-Sea. Although the records for this particular Hampshire-registered vehicle (AA 768) have been carelessly destroyed, it is believed that the operator was named John Lance. He ran a daily service between Milford-on-Sea and Lymington, leaving from the Crown hotel, Milford, at 9.20a.m., 10.50, 1.00, 3.00, 5.30 and 7.00p.m. The return journeys departed from the Lymington Town railway station at 10.40a.m., 12.35, 3.05 and 7.20p.m. On this particular occasion the vehicle was full to capacity, with two passengers seated beside the driver and five in each of the three benches behind him. The total number of persons riding is eighteen.

Following page, bottom: An early Winchester saloon omnibus, 1906. Here we can see a 14hp Maudslay with a single-deck omnibus body, believed to have been assembled and fitted at the Great Western Railway road motor works in Swindon. The chassis was manufactured at the Parkside factory of the Maudslay Motor Company Limited, in Coventry. A sliding door was fitted on the nearside of the driver's seat, through which the passengers could gain entry to the saloon. A maximum of fourteen persons could be seated inside. A ladder was provided at the back of the cabin for access to the luggage area on the roof.

The first Sandbanks motor omnibus service, 1905. This 20hp canopied charabanc was allocated the Bournemouth registration mark El 316 ton 17 August 1905. Manufactured by the De Dion Bouton company of Paris, it was operated by the Sandbanks Motor Car Company Limited, of 27 Fish Street, Poole. At the time of the photograph the carriage was painted yellow and blue. It also had blue Pegamoid side curtains and blue leather upholstery. In February 1913 a Commercar Torpedo charabanc replaced the De Dion Bouton, the fate of which has not been recorded.

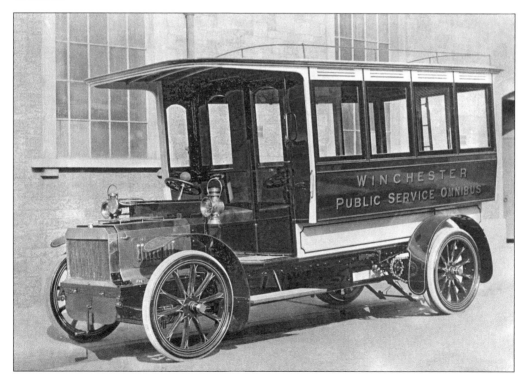

A Commercar estate bus at Milton Abbas, Dorset in 1908. This 18hp, chain-driven Commercar does not seem to fit perfectly into any particular category – the picture could easily have been represented in several other sections of this book. It is not a bus and yet it could carry fourteen persons. It is not a lorry, although it often carried goods. It is really too large to be a car, but it could easily be described as an estate car or a shooting brake. The vehicle was allocated the Dorset mark FX 141 on 10 March 1908. It was the second issue of the mark. Previously it applied to a dark claret-coloured Chelmsford Brake of 1904 vintage. Both vehicles were owned by Everard Alexander Hambro of Milton Abbas. For much of its life, as on this particular occasion, the Commercar brake was used to transport the gentlemen members of shooting parties. The chassis and the natural wood-grained body were manufactured by Commercial Cars Limited at Luton. A well-respected maker of the time, their later products just carried the name Commer.

Following page, bottom: Holidaymakers on a charabanc outing to Corfe Castle in July 1912. This odd-looking machine is a 35hp De Dion Bouton red-coloured charabanc, named *Lizzie II*. Registered with the Dorset mark FX 1546, she was one of a fleet of three similar vehicles operated by Mrs Annie Poulain of the Haven Hotel, Parkstone. *Lizzie III* (painted in a chocolate colour) can also be seen here before setting off from Bournemouth on the four-shilling return trip to Corfe Castle, via Wareham. She carried the mark FX 1080. The third machine, *Lizzie I* (FX 2139), is not seen in this picture postcard, produced by the Bournemouth View Company Limited of St Paul's Lane, Bournemouth.

A Thornycroft bus on an outing to the ancient stones of Wiltshire, 1911. Pictured here at Stonehenge on 18 August 1911 is a party of day trippers from Avonshire. Their conveyance carries the Bristol registration mark AE 733. Originally based in Chiswick, John I. Thornycroft & Company later built a wide range of cars, steam lorries, buses and commercial vehicles at their works in Basingstoke, Hampshire. Sadly, production ceased there in 1973.

An Aldershot and District Thornycroft at the Falcon Inn, Fawley. The Hampshire mark AA 2139 was allocated to this Thornycroft, type 80, single-deck omnibus on 4 July 1912. A hand-written note on the back of the original photograph states that it was the first motor vehicle to have been employed by the Aldershot and District Motor Traction Syndicate. The picture was taken sometime later, when the vehicle had passed into the hands of the London and South Western Railway Company. The licensee of the Falcon Inn at that time was Arthur Waterman.

Following page, bottom: The Chitterne bus on a day trip to Ringwood, 1913. At the time of the photograph there were several businesses being run by members of the Polden family in the Wiltshire village of Chitterne. Bertram and Edward Polden were farmers; Polden and Feltham were blacksmiths, carpenters and undertakers; the Polden Brothers were masons; and Sidney Polden was the village carrier. There was also the Polden motor service which ran to Salisbury Market and back on Tuesday and Saturday every week. During the summer months their Alldays and Onions charabanc (AM 3084) was often to be seen carrying a party of day trippers to Bournemouth, Weymouth or Southsea. The Alldays is shown here in front of George Hext's watchmakers' shop in the High Street at Ringwood.

A Commercar from Cranborne Mews, before the First World War. Here we can see a 35hp Commercar WP model parked outside Hankinson's Chambers in Bournemouth (Hankinson & Son was established in 1865). The photograph can be precisely dated to the spring of 1913, as there are a number of posters displayed in the windows promoting auctions to be held in June of that year. This green-coloured conveyance (EL 1520) was purchased by Albert Walker Futcher of Cranborne Mews, Tregonwell Road, Bournemouth, in October 1912. Two years later, in July 1914, the vehicle was sold to The Stevens Char-a-Banc Company (O.J. Stevens, S.W. Cotte, A.J. Pratt and A.E. Ball, proprietors) of the Isle of Purbeck Garage, Swanage.

A photo opportunity for 'Little Tich' at Bournemouth in 1914. This pretty little De Dion Bouton torpedo charabanc was named after the celebrated dwarfish music hall comedian Harry Ralph (1868-1928) who was popularly known as Little Tich. You can just see the name sign-written on the back of the body. The powder-blue vehicle was registered with the mark EL 1718 on 14 May 1914. Its operator was Walter Dinnivan of 48 Poole Road, Westbourne, Bournemouth. In July 1915 ownership was transferred to the Elliott Brothers' Royal Blue fleet.

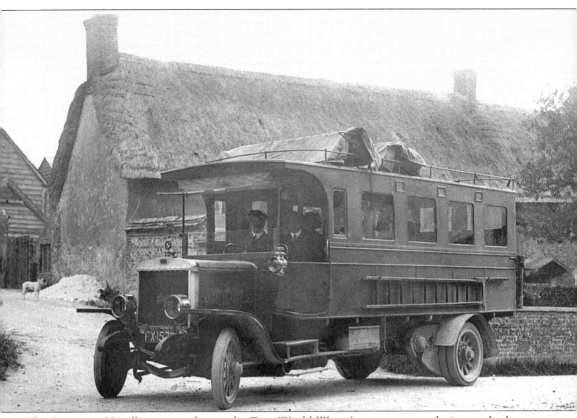

The Sixpenny Handley carrier during the First World War. A transport revolution took place in Wessex during the second decade of the twentieth century. For hundreds of years country carriers had been ferrying passengers and produce between town and village in horse-drawn vehicles that were primarily designed for carrying goods. In 1911, the Salisbury based Scout Motor Company (Clifford Herbert Radcliffe, Albert Thomas Burden and William Burden, directors) supplied a motor van to Victor White of Hurstbourne Tarrant, Hampshire. The vehicle was an instant success, offering levels of speed, comfort and convenience that had not been possible with a horse and cart. Operators from across the region ordered the new machines. In March 1913, Harold Roy Bartley took delivery of this olive-brown 25.6hp Scout carriers van (FX 1578) which ran regularly between Sixpenny Handley and Salisbury. On many of the Scout machines the top half of the body could be removed to form a low-sided platform lorry that was ideal for carrying hay and straw. With the top in place, but the internal bench seats removed, the vehicle was perfect for house removals. In fine weather, passengers could choose to ride on the roof (not for the faint-hearted), but on this particular occasion the benches were covered up. The stepladder can be seen on the body. Mark Burgess was the driver.

Previous page, bottom: An LGOC torpedo charabanc in Weymouth, 1916. Originally presented as a mahogany-bodied, double-deck, B-type omnibus, this vehicle was part of the London General Omnibus Company fleet. On 3 February 1916, having been sold to an operator based at Overdale House, Holly Road, Westham, Weymouth (the new owner may have been named Edward William Puffett), the vehicle was re-registered with the Dorset mark FX 2581. The double-deck bodywork was removed in September 1916 and a new torpedo body was fitted to the chassis. Here a party of day trippers can be seen, about to set off from St Thomas Street in Weymouth. George Fudge's ironmongers' shop and the Labour Exchange can be seen in the background.

The 'Winchester Wanderer' about to depart to the New Forest in 1919. This unusual-looking vehicle is based on a 20hp Ford Model T, the chassis of which had been extended by the British and American Import Company (Baico Patents Limited) of The Hyde, London. Vehicles converted like this were marketed as the *Baico/Ford Extendatonna*. It can be clearly seen that the vehicle featured side-chain final drive. Redman and Company, of the City Garage, Winchester, was the first operator of this particular conveyance. It was allocated the Southampton mark CR 2983 on 26 April 1916. Four years later, on 12 March 1920, ownership was transferred to Henry James Coombes, of Durngate Garage, Winchester. By 1 December 1920, the charabanc body had been removed and a slate-coloured, hinge-sided, platform body was bolted to the chassis. The lorry ended its days in Hampshire with James Ernest Hedgecock of Finchdean, Horndean.

Following page, *bottom*: A Wilts and Dorset omnibus on the Salisbury to Wilton service, March 1921. Pictured here in Bridge Street, Salisbury, is an AEC (3-ton) YC chassis with Tilling double-deck bodywork. The first purchase order for vehicles by Wilts and Dorset Motor Services after the First World War comprized seven machines: two single-deck buses (AEC/Dodson CD 3177 and AEC/Dodson CD 5248), two charabancs (AEC/Harrington, CD 3330 and Leyland/Harrington CD 5247) and three double-deckers (AEC/Brush CD 2555, Leyland/Dodson CD 2556 and the vehicle pictured to the right, AEC/Tilling CD 5249).

A government double-deck omnibus at Blandford camp, in 1919. Supplied by the Secretary of State for War for use at Station 85, RAF Blandford, the vehicle was allocated the Dorset mark FX 4430 on 4 March 1919. Based on the AEC 3-ton YC type chassis, the vehicle was painted in service colours. The front end of a Hampshire-registered Leyland RAF tender (HO 7007) can just be seen on the right.

A Hants and Dorset bus on a return service to Bournemouth, March 1921. Here we can see one of three 40hp, Leyland single-deck buses to have been registered on 30 November 1920. The trio comprised EL 4574, EL 5553 and EL 5554. All the machines were painted green and sign-written in the livery of the Hants and Dorset Motor Services Limited, of The Royal Mews, Norwich Avenue, Bournemouth. Departing from its stand beside the Queen Street shop of Woodrow and Son (corn, seed, cake and manure merchants) in Salisbury, the bus travelled back to Bournemouth via Fordingbridge, Ringwood and Christchurch.

Following page, bottom: A party of Southampton day trippers take a ride in a Dennis torpedo, 1923. Formerly operating as two independent fleets, the Hiawatha and Queen enterprise was run by William Aloysius Browne of Copsewood Road, Bitterne Park. (Later he was to become a herbalist, based at 134 St Mary Street, Southampton.) There were AEC, Crossley and Dennis vehicles in the fleet, when this photograph was taken in front of the Temperance and Commercial Hotel at 21 Canal, Salisbury. Like so many other charabancs of the 1920s, this particular Dennis machine was originally supplied as a 'subsidy' model for the transportation of goods during the First World War.

A Hampshire shopfitters' outing to Larmer Tree, in around 1922. Here we can see one of the numerous torpedo charabancs from Elliott Brothers' Royal Blue fleet. This AEC machine is unusual in having a large luggage container fitted at the rear. This was almost certainly a later modification and it would not have been shown on the original coachbuilder's drawings. Issued with the Bournemouth mark EL 3607 in April 1919, the vehicle carried fleet number ten. On this particular day it was accompanied by two other Royal Blue motors (Daimler/5b – EL 3788 and Daimler/1c – EL 4943) that had been hired by D. Drake and Son (shopfitters) of Orchard Lane, Bournemouth, for their annual staff outing.

Charabanc heaven at Trowbridge in 1924. On the left of the front rank we can see the cream and black 25/30hp Crossley (HR 6252) operated by Gerald Graham Stamper of The Garage, St Margaret Street, Bradford-on-Avon. He has twelve passengers seated. Next in line is an AEC torpedo model (HR 3193) with a full compliment of twenty-eight riders. This conveyance was hired from Crook and Sons of New Broughton Road, Melksham. The firm ran a well-presented fleet of blue-coloured charabancs. Next in line is a cream-painted Daimler, carrying the Somerset registration mark Y 5430, which is believed to have come from Frome. The AEC twenty-eight seater(YA 922), standing in the right foreground, was operated by the National Omnibus Company of Brompton Road, London. It possibly carries their fleet number 2006. Unfortunately, we can see no identifiable features on the three charabancs parked in the second row. Coming into view in the background is Trowbridge Town Hall (officially opened by the Duchess of Albany on 14 June 1899), in front of which stands a Bristol saloon bus in the livery of the Bath Tramways Motor Company Limited. On this particular day it was running on the Bradford and Bath service. The postcard photograph was produced by Houlton Brothers of 11 Fore Street, Trowbridge.

Following page, bottom: A Daimler from Dorset, running on Goodyear balloon tyres, 1926. This smartly turned out conveyance takes us into the era of the pneumatic tyre that did so much to improve the ride on private and public service vehicles. Operated by Weymouth Motor Company Limited (WMC), this machine was allocated the Dorset mark FX 5962 on 21 July 1920. It was one of several similar WMC Daimler charabancs to be seen running around Weymouth at that time – there was also FX 5523, FX 5836, and FX 6061. Depending on your point-of-view, the driver of FX 5962 on this particular day was unlucky to have been carrying an all-female party, as a drop of ale was unlikely to have passed his lips all day. The photograph was taken by Harold Whitworth. The front entrances to the Central Toilet Saloon and Roe Buck Inn were to be found in Butcher Row, Salisbury. Here we can see the back of the buildings in Canal.

A Thornycroft double-decker on service around Portsmouth, in 1925. Taken on 5 May, the photograph shows vehicle No.10 from the Portsmouth Corporation Tramways fleet. The open-top, double-deck body is fitted to a Thornycroft J type chassis that was assembled in Basingstoke at the time of the First World War. A large number were made. The Portsmouth Tramways depot was in Hester Road, Eastney at that time. Ben Hall was Chief Engineer and General Manager.

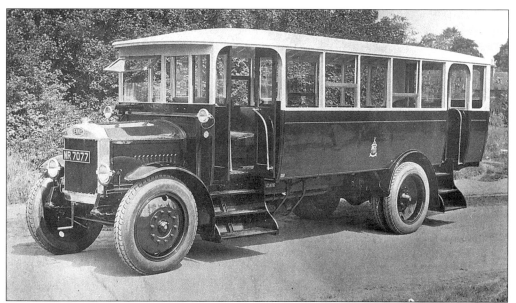

A coffee and cream-coloured conveyance in north Wiltshire, 1926. Here we can see a Dennis dual-entry bus (MR 7077) registered by Albert Rimes of the Swindon Motor Charabanc Company on 14 July 1926. The 40hp machine carried chassis No.40411C and engine No.18502. It was manufactured in Guildford.

A Hants and Dorset bus on a service to Calshot in 1928. The green-painted vehicle can be seen here passing through The Square in Fawley. It is an L-series Leyland that was allocated the Bournemouth mark RU 5796 on 27 July 1927.

A Reo Speedwagon visiting Gough's Caves at Cheddar in 1928. The chassis of this grey and red-coloured machine was manufactured by the Reo Motor Car Company of Lansing, Michigan, USA, but the charabanc body is believed to have been assembled and fitted locally. It was operated by Messrs Clothier and Hayward of Spring Road, Bournemouth. The Borough of Bournemouth motor taxation office issued the registration mark RU 5466 on 4 June 1927.

A Wilts and Dorset bus returns to Salisbury, 1928. The picture shows the first of a batch of three 28.9hp Leyland PLSC3 models and a Dennis G type acquired by Wilts and Dorset Motor Services Limited of Salisbury. On 24 February 1928, the machines were allocated consecutive Wiltshire registration marks MW 1851 to MW 1854. Operated as fleet No.55, this particular machine carried Leyland's chassis No.47128. The thirty-six-seat, rear-entry bodywork was likewise assembled at the Leyland factory. Here it is displaying destination boards for Service 3 – Salisbury to Bournemouth, via Fordingbridge and Ringwood.

A Reo Pullman on a return service to Southampton in the late 1920s. Here we can see the green and black-coloured saloon bus that was operated by John King of Nomansland, Wiltshire. It was registered at Trowbridge on 28 September 1926 and the 25hp vehicle was allocated the mark MR 7958. It had chassis No.2556 and engine No.2150A. The bodywork was designed to transport twenty passengers in relative comfort.

The Fordingbridge 'Victory' bus of 1931. Very little has been recorded about this particular coach, which is based on a Thornycroft CCL chassis. With a wheelbase of 16ft 6in, the machine was powered by a 40.6hp, six-cylinder petrol engine. The attractive two-tone bodywork carries the mark of Lee Motor Works (Bournemouth) Limited, whose workshops were to be found in Wimborne Road, Bournemouth. The vehicle was allocated the Hampshire mark OU 8577 on 24 April 1931. Its registered keeper was one Austin W. Alner (trading as Victory Coaches), The Myrtles, Park Road, Fordingbridge. Is that him standing here?

Previous page, bottom: An AEC Reliance coach with Duple bodywork for Royal Blue. Between 25 March and 3 June 1929, Elliott Brothers (Bournemouth) Limited took delivery of twenty-five coaches, each with twenty-eight, thirty or thirty-two seats fitted. The vehicle shown here is a twenty-eight-seat model (RU 8807) which, along with seven other machines from the same batch, was sold to Southern National on 1 January 1935. Allocated fleet No.3712, the machine was later fitted with a twenty-eight-seat Beadle body. It was sold out of service in 1948.

A photo opportunity for a Leyland Titan at Dilton Marsh in 1933. This lake and ivory-coloured double-decker was registered in Wiltshire on 30 June 1931. Operated by the Western National Omnibus Company Limited of Brompton Road, London, it was given Leyland's chassis No. TD1/72030. It was fitted with Leyland's new 6.8 litre (38/40hp) petrol engine. More than 2,300 Titans were produced between 1927 and 1931.

A Dennis Ace that took to the roads of the Isle of Wight in 1934. At the time of this photograph an average of fifty-five vehicles a month were being allocated an Isle of Wight DL registration mark. The series had been running since December 1903. DL 9015 was issued on 18 June 1934 for use on this particular Harrington-bodied Dennis Ace bus, which was car number 405 in the Southern Vectis fleet. The machine is now preserved by an enthusiast. The photograph was taken by C. Carter.

Poole's new baby, a fortnight old and doing fine, 1935. This young lad, with his Hants and Dorset hat and dust-coat, won First Prize in Class II of the 1935 Poole Carnival. His model was representative of the Leyland Titans, that had just taken over the Poole to Bournemouth services, via North Road and Ashley Road, from the Bournemouth Corporation Transport trams. An authentic sign-written advertisement for Bobby's shop and restaurant can be seen on the side of the model.

An Albion Victor coach in service around Southampton, 1936. Mr E.L. Easson was proprietor of Easson's Motor Garage (motor coach operators) of 179 Spring Road, Sholing. Here we can see his Albion Victor, model PK114, on a service to Hedge End and Woolston. The Southampton mark ACR 391 was issued in August 1936.

Dennis Lance low-height double-deckers for Aldershot, 1937. The Aldershot and District Motor Traction Company Limited (A & D) took delivery of forty-one Dennis low-bridge buses in the summer of 1937. They were issued with consecutive Hampshire registration marks – CCG 311-351. The bodies, made by Strachan, were designed to carry forty-eight passengers (twenty-two on the lower deck and twenty-six on the upper deck). Here we can see car No.722 (CCG 319) which is about to depart on service 3A to Cove, via Aldershot North Camp, Farnborough Town Hall and Victoria Road. As far as we know not one of the Lance double-deckers from this batch has survived. There are, however, several preserved examples of later A & D Dennis buses.

Previous page, bottom: A star that shone brightly in Wessex for forty years. The Silver Star motor service was launched by E.W. 'Eddie' Shergold and B.F. 'Ben' White in 1923. From its base at Porton Camp, the firm ran services to the city of Salisbury and the military centres on Salisbury Plain. In May 1936 a Leyland Tiger coach (model TS7) was acquired, to which was allocated the Wiltshire mark AAM 756. Originally fitted with a half-cabbed Burlingham body, the machine was later re-modelled by Heaver Limited, at their coach-building works in Bulford Road, Durrington. The vehicle, with its new full-fronted appearance, carrying fleet No.23, can be seen here passing R.R. Edwards' premises in Castle Street, Salisbury.

A new Bedford Duple for Bournemouth Corporation, 1937. This is an official photograph produced by Duple Bodies and Motors Limited, of The Hyde, London. It was taken before the vehicle was handed over to Duncan P. Morrison, the General Manager of Bournemouth Corporation Transport Services. Based on the Bedford WTB passenger chassis, the twenty-five-seat, sun-saloon coach was allocated the Borough of Bournemouth registration mark DEL 657 in May 1937.

A Dodge destined for the Isle of Wight, in1939. This attractive Dodge coach was first operated by Nash's Motor Coaches of 122/123 Pier Street, Ventnor. The twenty-five-seat all-weather bodywork is believed to have been produced by Reading and Company Limited, of London Road, Hillsea, Portsmouth. It is based on a Dodge RBF chassis that had been supplied by J.H. Sparshatt & Sons (Portsmouth) Limited. The Isle of Wight registration mark CDL 96 was issued on Monday 11 April 1938. Sparshatt & Sons, and several other Portsmouth-based commercial vehicle bodybuilders, often employed Messrs Wright and Logan, of Albert Road, Southsea, to take photographs of new vehicles. The quality of their work is clear for all to see.

Five
Lorries, Trucks and Vans

An early 8hp Daimler van for carrying fish and poultry. Mrs Priscilla Hart purchased this two-cylinder Daimler in February 1906, at which time it received the Wiltshire mark AM 764. It was manufactured in 1903, but there is no known record of the vehicle's early history. Solid rubber tyres were fitted to the front and rear wheels, and final drive was by side chains. Influenced by the horse-drawn era, the general layout of this vehicle afforded very little consideration for the driver, or carman, as he would then have been known – there are no doors or windscreens fitted around the driving compartment. The cabinet-style photograph was produced by Horace 'Charlie' Messer, of Castle Street, Salisbury.

A Beaufort motor trolley, working in Westbury, Wiltshire, 1908. Based in Baden, Germany, the Beaufort Motor Company set up a UK sales office in a small passage off Baker Street, London. The Warminster Motor Company was their appointed concessionaire for the Wessex region. Over a period of seven years (1901-1908) they may have sold fewer than twenty Beaufort vehicles. (They were far more successful with their Humber franchise.) Of the few commercial vehicles supplied this one would appear to have the longest wheelbase. Allocated the Wiltshire mark AM 1121 on 2 January 1908, the 10/12hp trolley was supplied to A. Laverton and Company (woollen and worsted manufacturers) of Westbury Mill. Driven through a live axle, the vehicle ran with solid rubber bands on the rear wheels and pneumatic tyres on the front. The body sides of this lead-coloured vehicle could be removed to provide a flat loading platform. An 11cwt load could be carried in relative safety.

Following page, bottom: An advertisement for a new De Dion 10cwt van that took to the streets of Southampton in 1907. The Parsons Motor Company Limited, of Town Quay, Southampton, supplied this smart-looking delivery car to Mr W.J. Rich, baker and confectioner, in October 1907. The body was constructed by Messrs Hale and Pearce of 22 Lower Bannister Street, Southampton (the firm also had a coach-building workshop at 91 Bedford Place). The 9hp De Dion was finished in a dark shade of blue, with silver sign-writing and silver coach-lining – a very smart combination. It would seem that Mr Rich was delighted with his van because in January and February 1908 a picture of it was published in Commercial Motor magazine. "the van is giving great satisfaction," he wrote.

A Royal Mail delivery to Bridport Post Office in Dorset, 1908. Pictured here, in front of the Post Office in East Street, is a 20hp Gladiator van, operated by George Louis Banfield. Based at 66 West Street, Bridport, he had been the local contractor to the Royal Mail for many years. This particular conveyance was painted dark blue, and there were fine white lines giving detail to the wings, wheels and engine cover. Having been allocated the Dorset mark FX 420 on 5 February 1908, the Gladiator had been replaced by a Model T Ford by 1 September 1920. Mr Banfield had transferred the FX 420 mark to the new machine.

Southampton's latest motorvan (De Dion chassis).

A rare, swiss-made Orion motor wagon working in Salisbury in 1909. Victor James Blew was an official parcel-carrying agent for the Great Western Railway Company, in Salisbury; he was also a coal merchant and a removal contractor. On this particular occasion his men were removing the contents of George Brown's house in Hulse Road, Salisbury. (If the furniture was to be transported some distance the box container would probably have been lifted off the lorry by a steam crane and lowered onto a railway truck.) The Orion was originally supplied as one of a small number of experimental double-deck omnibuses ordered by the London General Omnibus Company Limited. The vehicles proved to be unsuitable and were later sold. Mr Blew acquired one of them, and after removal of the passenger bodywork a drop-sided float body was fitted to the chassis. The refurbished machine was assigned the Wiltshire registration mark AM 1411 on 14 May 1909.

Following page, bottom: A Commercar carries booze around Bournemouth, 1913. This 22hp, chain-driver Commercar MC model first took to the road with Henry Newman and Company Limited of 3 Lansdowne Crescent, Bournemouth. Its blue-coloured body foundation was topped with a white canvas cover. The vehicle was allocated the Bournemouth mark EL 1946 on 29 December 1913. It was one of Commercar's smallest vehicles.

Meat by motor for the military men on manoeuvres, 1911. Throughout the early years of the twentieth century, Messrs Webb and Wilson were fortunate to have been awarded many contracts to supply fresh meat and poultry to the numerous officers messes established around the army camps of west Hampshire and the northern parts of Salisbury Plain. From their retail outlet at 11 Bridge Street, Andover, the firm ran a small fleet of delivery vehicles including a three-wheeled Autocarrier which carried the Hampshire registration mark AA 3280. They also ordered two vans from the Salisbury-based Scout Motor Company Limited, one of which can be seen here. Both machines were Model 10K Scouts, that would carry a 10cwt load. The specification of the 10K included a four-cylinder, 18-22hp engine, three speeds and live axle transmission.

From Grove City, Pennsylvania to Trowbridge, Wiltshire, in 1915. Here we can see an imported chain-driven Bessemer truck employed by J.H. and H. Blake (brewers, wine and spirit merchants and maltsters) of 18-19 Union Street, Trowbridge. The Wiltshire mark AM 5171 was set aside for the machine on 9 July 1915. Records show that it was a 2½ton model (chassis No.858) that was powered by a 36hp, four-cylinder, Continental engine (No.14524C). The brewer's dray body was painted red and there were fine black lines applied to the wings, wheels, engine cover and cab. By 1923, the vehicle had found a new owner – J. Clifford of 75 Lower Bristol Road, Bath. The Bessemer Motor Truck Company, of Grove City, manufactured commercial vehicles from 1911 to 1923, but relatively few chassis were exported to Great Britain.

Following page, bottom: An example of local loyalty in Basingstoke, 1921. Based in Essex Road, the Co-operative Society was keen to support local trade and it purchased this 2½ton, BT-type delivery van (chassis No.8669) from John I. Thornycroft and Company Limited, of Worting Road, Basingstoke. The vehicle was allocated the Hampshire registration mark HO 5546 on Monday 8 August 1921. The upper part of the van body could be taken off in one piece.

A Ford Model T brewer's dray working in Weymouth, 1920. The Model T Ford is arguably the most well known vehicle of all time. Although it has appeared in countless guises all around the world, the marque was not often to be found working as a brewer's dray. Messrs John Grove and Sons, of Hope Brewery, Weymouth, registered this blue-coloured example on 1 October 1920. It was allocated the Dorset mark FX 6254.

A 'Park's of Portsmouth' takes a dive in Dorset, 1925. Any knowledge of the events leading up to this incident remain hidden in the mists of time, but thankfully some forward-thinking individual had scribbled a few details on the back of the original picture. This is one of George Park's Leylands, a 30hp, three or four-ton model, hanging over Durweston Bridge. Dating from the time of the First World War, the truck was not registered until 1924. It was allocated the Portsmouth mark TP 924 on 18 December. Park (George) and Company Limited, of 182-184 Albert Road, Southsea, operated a large fleet of lorries, trucks and vans. Throughout the 1920s, the firm ran a series of advertisements using the slogan 'A Hundred Vans and Acres of Storage'. Published as a photographic postcard, the original picture carries the imprint of Lloyd Stickle, commercial photographer, of 7 Damory Street, Blandford.

Following page, bottom: A Trojan sunbathing in Swanage, 1927. Mr E.Y. Coombes of 'Springfield', Victoria Avenue, Swanage, took delivery of this odd-looking machine in February 1927. It was allotted the Dorset mark PR 7694. The van is typical of the extraordinary vehicles produced by Trojan Limited, of Croydon, in the late 1920s and early 1930s. It had a four-cylinder two-stroke engine and chain drive. By choosing not to have pneumatic tyres fitted to his van Mr Coombes saved £5. Trojan promoted the solid rubber tyred option because they supposedly lasted twice as long. Thankfully, Trojans had very soft suspension.

Doing the rounds in the historic Wiltshire village of Avebury, 1926. Here we can see a Ford Model T van (HR 7134) finished in the livery of William Thomas Cooper, baker and grocer. The foundation colour of the bodywork was midnight blue, with grey sign-writing. Rated at 7cwts, the vehicle was marked with Ford's chassis and engine No.5827024. Is this Mr Cooper and his wife pictured out on the rounds?

A Scammell eight-wheeler for Southern Roadways, 1928. The motive unit of this impressive-looking commercial vehicle was manufactured by Scammell Lorries Limited, of Watford. It is an example of their LW24 tractor that was powered by a four-cylinder petrol engine. Introduced in 1920, the model was originally fitted with solid rubber tyres, but large balloon tyres became popular for long distance haulage work in the late twenties. Carrying a twelve-ton load, the vehicle was limited to a maximum speed of 16mph. The semi-trailer was manufactured by Lee Motor Works (Bournemouth) Limited, of Wimborne Road, Bournemouth. The operators, Southern Roadways, of West Shore Wharf, Poole, were road haulage contractors to Bladen Dairies at the time. The firm had reserved four Dorset registration marks in 1927. TK 1000 and TK 1001 were allocated to a pair of Leyland trucks, and TK 1002 was allotted to the Scammell articulated eight-wheeler seen here. The fourth mark, TK 1003, appears never to have been used.

Following page, bottom: Leyland truck and trailer travels around Hampshire, 1930. This truck is one of a pair of Leyland GH6 models purchased by White & Company Limited, of 71 High Street, Southampton, in May 1930. The machines were allocated the Southampton marks TR 8736 and TR 8737 (shown here). The chassis, supplied by the Portsmouth Commercial Motor Company Limited, were fitted with bodies manufactured by J.H. Sparshatt & Sons (Portsmouth) Limited. There are several features in the photograph that are worthy of our attention. The truck's fuel supply was carried in cans stored amidships under the bodywork on the near side, and the trailer was originally an independent, horse-drawn unit. The driver's seat and footrest are still evident on the front of the box-van.

Morris moves milk around Andover, 1928. The Managing Secretary of The Andover Co-operative Society Limited, Edwin Thorogood, registered this Morris Commercial milk float on 27 November 1928. It was allocated the Hampshire mark OU 186. Based on the L type (12cwt) chassis, the vehicle carries a curtain-sided float body, assembled and fitted at Charles Jerome's coachworks, at 57 Chantry Street, Andover. The colour scheme comprised a dark blue foundation with cream features and powder blue, sign-written lettering, which had a dark blue outline, where necessary. The illuminated sign box above the cab was manufactured by the Franco Sign Company.

Dennis side-tipping trucks for Wiltshire County Council, 1931. The Wiltshire County Surveyor (Howard Sims Ganderton, of Bradford-on-Avon) ordered four 30cwt trucks from Dennis Brothers of Guildford. The machines were allocated the consecutive Wiltshire registration marks WV 81 to WV 84 (chassis Nos 56471, 56470, 56467 and 56482 respectively). It seems that all four tippers were broken up by the end of the Second World War, but at least two of the registration numbers may still be in use today. In March 1951, Mr W.V. Whitehouse-Vaux, of Mount Park Crescent, London, successfully persuaded an officer of Wiltshire County Council to authorize the transfer of the expired mark WV 81. Upon payment of £5, the mark was reissued for use on an AC car. It was all quite legal at that time. Today a registration number such as WV 81 could change hands for several thousand pounds. If only we'd known then what we know now!

Following page, bottom: A Thornycroft selected to collect rubbish on the Isle of Wight, 1933. Here we can see just one of the numerous Thornycroft 'AA Forward' low-height chassis that were used by local authorities for refuse collection work in the Wessex region in the 1930s. The model preferred by the Transport Department of Ryde Borough Council was the 12cu yd 'Eagle' collector, manufactured by the Eagle Engineering Company Limited of Warwick. Its container has foot-operated dust covers for side loading. The Isle of Wight mark DL 8485 was issued for use on this machine in June 1933.

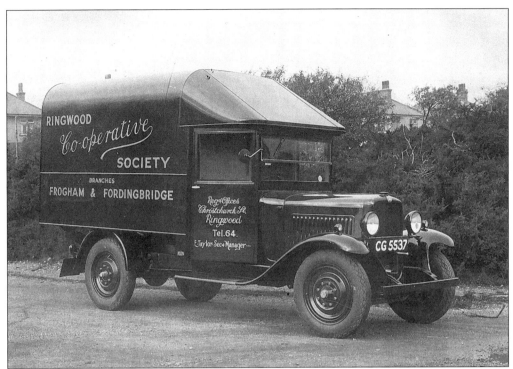

The Ringwood Co-operative Society purchased this Bedford van in 1933. Supplied by Lee Motors (Bournemouth) Limited, the Bedford WS type van was allocated the Hampshire mark CG 5537 on Friday 14 April 1933. Rated at 30cwts, the WS model made its debut in 1931. With a wheelbase of 131 inches, and powered by a 23.6hp, six-cylinder petrol engine, it was a very popular vehicle in its day.

A white Bedford for the Whiting works at Wilton, 1935. This is an example of the short-wheelbase version of Bedford's three-ton chassis, the WTH. Howard C. Cooke registered this particular one for E.H. Cooke and Son, of Wilton, on Tuesday 19 March 1935. Issued with the Wiltshire mark WV 7436, it carried Bedford's chassis No.861214. By 1 April 1942 the truck had been sold to Bert Rusher of 15 Meadow Cottages, The Friary, Salisbury. The photograph was taken by F. Lindsey of Trowbridge.

An Albion arrives at a Portsmouth pub with Brickwoods Best Bitter, 1936. This sturdy-looking Albion Model 53, with dropside bodywork, is believed to have been acquired by W.G. Privett of Drayton Lane, Cosham, in November 1937. It was allocated the Portsmouth mark RV 9229. The truck was employed on contract work for Brickwood and Company Limited of Admiral Road, Portsmouth.

A Dodge in Dorset, 1937. The main Dodge agent in the Wessex region, for many years, was J.H. Sparshatt & Sons (Portsmouth) Limited, of London Road, Hillsea. Registered with the Dorset mark JT 7328, they supplied this 40cwt RS Model to Arthur Janes (Saddler and Harness maker), of Bere Regis, on 28 May 1937. The stake-sided bodywork was designed for general agricultural duties, including the transportation of livestock. The photograph was produced by Wright and Logan, of Albert Road, Southsea.

A Reo Speedwagon used for bulk milk deliveries around Southampton, 1938. Powered by a Reo Gold Crown engine, this four-ton, semi-forward control truck was supplied by George Dear, of Whiteparish. As the main Reo concessionaire for Hampshire and Wiltshire, he sold the machine to Model Dairies Limited (Stanley G Harrison, managing director). The chain-sided float body was assembled and fitted by Longman Brothers (cart, van and wagon builders) at their works in Redbridge, Southampton. The Wiltshire mark BAM 942 was issued on 31 January 1931. The photograph carries the imprint of F. Futcher and Son, 19 Fisherton Street, Salisbury.

An AEC Monarch cattle truck in north Wiltshire, 1939. Austin Clarke & Sons (Minety) Limited were loyal users of AEC vehicles throughout the 1930s and 1940s. This particular one is a diesel-engined Monarch 344 model that carried the Borough of Bournemouth mark ERU 249. The vehicle was registered on 1 January 1939 by the agent and bodybuilder, Lee Motor Works (Bournemouth) Limited, of Wimborne Road, Bournemouth, on behalf of their client. If the operator had applied to register the truck in Swindon then it would probably have been issued with a mark from the Wiltshire BMW or BWV series. From 1935 to 1946 Lee Motor Works produced three AEC cattle trucks for Austin Clarke – ARU 875 (Fleet No.8), ERU 249 (No.9) and EAM 583 (No.10).

Six

Emergency Service Vehicles

A steam fire engine and crew at Gillingham, Dorset in 1904. This was the scene in front of the Fire Engine House when a passing photographer stopped to take a snapshot of the town's volunteer firemen and their horse-drawn steamer. The crew had probably turned out for a Hydrant and Engine drill, which they did on a regular basis. Shand Mason & Company, of London, had supplied the appliance to the Gillingham Volunteer Fire Brigade in the late nineteenth century. The corrugated-iron clad fire station was still in use at the outbreak of the Second World War, by which time the brigade had upgraded to a Braidwood-style motor fire engine, named Lincoln. The sign above the fire station doors survived for very many years, but it was later re-written with the words Fire Station.

A Daimler fire tender for the Aldershot Volunteer Fire Brigade, 1911. This early motor tender is believed to have been based on an Edwardian, 30hp Daimler car chassis, that was later converted to a chemical appliance by Merryweather & Sons of Greenwich. The machine was allocated the Hampshire mark AA 3556. We can see that it carried a wheeled escape ladder and a 'first-aid' hose reel. A common feature of machines such as this was the large copper cylinder (of up to sixty gallons capacity) that was stored beneath, or to the rear, of the driver's seat.

A Dennis motor fire escape for the Borough of Bournemouth, 1913. This is an official Dennis Brothers' publicity photograph that, unfortunately, shows the vehicle before the application of its registration mark. We believe, however, that it is EL 1702, which was recorded in the Borough of Bournemouth 'Heavy Motor' register on 15 October 1913. The entry would suggest that the appliance carried a 50ft Ajax wheeled fire escape and a rear-mounted hose reel, but no water pumping facilities. Its specification included electric lighting, a bulb horn and a hand-operated warning bell. The Braidwood-designed body would seat a crew of six, as well as an officer and driver. A later photograph of the appliance shows that it was still in service in the mid-thirties.

Previous page, bottom: The Great Western Railway Company Fire Brigade at Swindon, 1912. This motor pump is typical of the fire appliances produced by Dennis Brothers of Guildford, in the early years of the twentieth century. Powered by a White and Poppe four-cylinder engine, the machine had a turbine water pump fitted at the rear. One interesting feature worth noting is the use of road chains on the rear wheels. The Wiltshire registration mark AM 2747 was set aside for the machine on Thursday 12 December 1912. The trailer pump is a conversion of an earlier Merryweather horse-drawn steam fire engine.

The new Codford camp motor fire engine, 1918. Soon after it arrived at Codford, this new Merryweather motor pump was pulled up in front of the fire station for an informal photograph to be taken with members of its crew. On 28 October 1918, the Secretary of State for War, provided the vehicle for government use at Codford military camp. It was assigned the Wiltshire registration mark AM 8940. The machine has wooden-spoked wheels fitted with solid rubber tyres, and it carried a 'first-aid' hose reel and a short extension ladder. Mounted at the back of the appliance was a Merryweather Hatfield pump, with a vertical air vessel. No record could be found of the vehicle's fate after it was taken out of service on Wednesday 21 February 1923.

Following page, bottom: A photo opportunity for Dorchester Fire Brigade in 1926. Here we can see a Leyland type FE1 motor fire engine near the fire station in Trinity Street, Dorchester. The appliance received the Dorset mark PR 6010 on 1 January 1926. A centrifugal pump was fitted at the rear of the machine, which had a capacity of 375 gallons per minute at 100lbs psi. The brigade was comprized of a captain (W Jewel), a second officer and ten firemen.

Trowbridge Urban District Council chose a Halley in 1923. Looking very smart indeed, with their new motor pump, are the men of Trowbridge and District Fire Brigade. Manufactured by Halley Industrial Motors Limited of Yoker, Glasgow, the Tylor-engined appliance was allocated the Wiltshire mark HR 8049 on Monday 19 March 1923. At the time the brigade comprized a captain (Walter Shaw), three officers and twelve firemen. The fire station stood in Castle Street.

A reconditioned Ford Model T, adopted by the Calne Fire Brigade in 1928. Powered by a 20hp, four-cylinder engine (Ford's No.10639099), this light commercial vehicle had a long and varied life. Having been allocated the Wiltshire mark MR 3514 on 20 April 1925, it was first put to work as a truck for the Calne Corporation Gas Department. It was painted grey. Then, in September 1928, the lorry was rebuilt as a fire tender for the Calne Fire Brigade (Frank Maundrell, Superintendent). One thing is very clear, this tiny fire appliance would not transport all the officers and firemen shown here. Most of the available space in the back of the vehicle had been taken up with fire-fighting apparatus, including a petrol-engined water pump, the top of which can just be seen in the picture.

Following page, bottom: One of numerous New World appliances to have arrived in Wessex by 1937. Although Braidwood fire appliances had been in use since the early 1800s, the design was fundamentally flawed. When sitting or standing along the side of a fire engine, many firemen were seriously injured or killed when they were thrown off a machine that was responding to an emergency call. The New World design, or Inside Type as it was sometimes called, was a great improvement on its predecessor, as it could accommodate the crew on inward-facing or forward-facing seats. Typical of the new age appliances, this elegant Dennis Big-Six pump escape was delivered to Gosport Fire Brigade in 1936.

Salisbury fire engines: 'The Chief' and 'The Chairman', made in 1933. Like many other brigades in Great Britain at that time, Salisbury Volunteer Fire Brigade ceremoniously adopted every new appliance that came into their service by giving it a name. Pictured here in front of the Salt Lane fire station are two Dennis machines: 'The Chief' (MW 6125), a Braidwood-styled motor-pump which was delivered in 1930, and the pump-escape named 'The Chairman' (WV 3993), that was christened in 1933. On the left we can see the Mayor of Salisbury, Councillor Mr Charles Scamell, standing between Alderman Sidney Rambridge and Chief Fire Officer L.G. Hardy.

An Auxiliary Fire Service oddity in Portsmouth, in 1939. J.H. Sparshatt and Sons (Portsmouth) Limited experimented with some very unusual vehicles for ARP and fire fighting purposes, in the years leading up to the Second World War. The two photographs on this page clearly show how a Packard Straight-Eight saloon had been converted for use by a local AFS unit.

The crossroads at Middle Wallop (A343 – Salisbury to Andover road) is believed to have been the site of the first speed trap operated by any police force in Great Britain. The drivers of the day knew the stretch of road only too well and journalists all over the country were writing about the 'Wallop Motor Trap'. A Wilton draper and gentlemen's outfitter named Fred Robinson even wrote a poem about it, which begins thus: 'Screened by the village wayside inn, The Hampshire Policemen stand, Watching Motor Cars come and go, With a stop-watch in their hands.' This picture shows a Napier car from the Hampshire constabulary parked beside the George Hotel in 1905. (The George was demolished in 1927). Pictured in the distance is Rose Hill House, which still stands today. The 30hp Napier was registered to the Chief Constable of Hampshire and it was allocated the Hampshire mark AA 108 in 1904. The speed limit at that time was set at just twenty miles per hour and policemen would crouch out of sight, with their stopwatches, recording the time that it took motor vehicles to travel between two points (a measured furlong). A local newspaper reported that the Andover bench raised more than £1000 in fines in a single year. That was a fortune in those days. The other car pictured here, turning left towards Over Wallop, is a 10/12hp royal-blue Beaufort tonneau that was first registered to Arthur Edwards (Managing Director of Edwards Brothers' garage in Salisbury). It carries the Wiltshire mark AM 544. At the time of this picture the car had passed into the hands of a new owner: John George Barlow Burry, of Ringwolde, Middle Wallop.

The Chief Constable's landaulette on the Isle of Wight, 1912. Here we can see the blue-coloured Standard car, registered to Captain Harry George Adams-Connor of The Rangers, Carter Street, Sandown. It was allocated the Isle of Wight mark DL 2146 in August 1912. There were no patrol cars as such employed by Wessex police forces at that time. There were a number of police ambulances in use around the area and a few Black Marias for transporting prisoners, but generally the only motor vehicles operated by police forces were cars that were used to ferry around high-ranking officers. Before 1920 it was common practice for the car to be registered in the name of the individual to whom it was allocated.

Following page, bottom: Traffic patrol cars in Dorset, 1935. The Dorset Constabulary purchased three cars in 1935: a Vauxhall (JT 3251), a Hillman (JT 3253) and an Austin (JT 3252), only two of which can be seen here. The cars were probably standard models, without any modifications. One could say that they came 'straight off the production line'. By 1939 the Dorset patrol car fleet had increased to thirteen, including several Ford Anglia models. Another interesting record from 1939 reveals that there were only three sets of traffic lights in the county at that time. They were to be found at Shaftesbury (a narrow street), at Lyme Regis (a narrow street) and at Ferndown.

A Portsmouth police car that came a cropper in the twenties. This 13.9hp Standard saloon would appear to be an SLO4 model, of which thousands were sold in Great Britain. It was a very popular car in its time This particular one is believed to have been allocated the Portsmouth mark BK 7994 early in 1923. It had been involved in an accident, as the front wing is badly damaged.

A Standard Flying Twelve for the Salisbury city police, 1937. The Salisbury City Constabulary purchased this 12hp car from their local Standard agent, S. & E. Collett of Catherine Street, Salisbury. It was allocated the Wiltshire mark BAM 834 on the last day of December 1937. Pictured here with the patrol car is Officer George Sleath. The photograph was taken by Harold Whitworth.

The Swindon police favoured an Austin Twelve in 1938. The car received the Wiltshire mark BMR 518 on Tuesday 9 August 1938. The vehicle registration form had been submitted by William Brooks, station officer of the Borough Police Station in Eastcott Road. The car was supplied by Skurray's Limited (automobile engineers) of 30/32 High Street, Swindon.

The Salisbury and District Isolation Hospital ambulance, 1912. The registration application for this 19.6hp motor ambulance was submitted to Wiltshire County Council by Francis Harding, who was at that time clerk of the Isolation Hospital at Old Sarum. The blue-coloured vehicle was manufactured by Scout Motors Limited of Salisbury. It was allocated the Wiltshire mark AM 2762 on 21 December 1912, and was the first motor ambulance to be seen on the roads of South Wiltshire.

A Morris ambulance for the Romsey and District Cottage Hospital, 1927. Beadle and Company of Dartford were the fabricators of this light-blue Morris Commercial ambulance. Having supplied the machine to the British Petroleum Company, it was issued with the Hampshire mark OT 4498. It had been registered by Capt, the Rt Hon C.K. Greenway on 11 April 1927. We have been unable to establish a connection between the Romsey and District Cottage Hospital, the British Petroleum Company and Lord Greenway. Perhaps you know the answer?

A handsome Talbot ambulance for the county of Dorset, 1934. A number of county and borough health authorities in the south of England operated this design of Talbot ambulance, designated the AY95. They were to be seen around Bristol, East Ham, Essex, Hampshire, Harrow, Kent, City of London, Penge, Surrey and Wiltshire. The Dorset Ambulance Service appears to have purchased just one machine in December 1934. The authority later acquired numerous Bedford chassis, several of which received bodywork fabricated at the Lee Motor Works in Wimborne Road, Winton.

The Portsmouth and Gosport Gas Company doing its bit in 1939. Functioning as a general service lorry during the day, this six-wheeled, Dennis Pax dropside truck was equipped to take on a very different role at night, fighting the flames of war with a local ARP contingent. A power take-off drove a pump, which forced water through spray heads mounted on the front of the vehicle, that were used to wash down the streets after a gas attack. Hoses could also be connected up for general fire-fighting duties, as shown here. A collapsible metal and wood cage, carried on the rear deck of the lorry, contained a large canvas water bag, an example of which is to be seen on the previous page.

Previous page, bottom: Sparshatt's Dennis to the rescue, in Portsmouth, 1938. This three-ton Dennis commercial recovery truck is lifting a bag of water that was being tested for leaks. The hand-operated crane, manufactured by Cook's Breakdown Equipment Company, seems almost to be bending under the strain. The Dennis lorry is also showing signs of exertion. Numerous heavy items, including railway sleepers and oil drums, had been stacked on the bonnet and wings to keep the front end down. The canvas water container, in action, can be seen in the above picture.

A Southampton ARP unit at the time of the Second World War. The motive unit of this articulated lorry is a Bedford W type, short-wheelbase model, introduced in 1931. It was fitted with a six-cylinder petrol engine (No.438177). In rigid form the model would carry two tons, but when fitted with a fifth wheel-coupling and a Carrimore semi-trailer it would accommodate a four-ton load, which was more than adequate for this representation of an ARP Intelligence Services bureau. The machine appears to be taking part in a National Services recruitment campaign. The lorry was registered by Mr J.A. Andrews, director of Andrews (Southampton) Limited, on 20 November 1932. It was allocated the Southampton mark OW 3999, a very distinctive number, for its new role in a national emergency service.

Following page, bottom: A tough Packard truck for the Army Service Corps in Wiltshire, 1916. This three-ton general service wagon was imported from the USA, with countless other types of military vehicles to help Great Britain fight her adversaries. It was delivered to 63 Company ASC, at Bulford on Salisbury Plain. Because of the large quantity of vehicles being registered in Wiltshire at the time of the First World War, the government sanctioned the use of a temporary registration scheme for military vehicles entering service at Bulford, using the mark BUL. Quite a number of photographs of those vehicles have survived. This particular one carries the mark BUL 2937. This real-photo postcard published by Phillipse and Lees shows Corporal Gates sitting on the toolbox.

An Austin rescue lorry that served with a Poole civil defence unit. The man pictured here is known simply as Bert. In 1942 he wrote home to his mother – 'Hope you will like this photograph of my Austin. Shall soon have to say goodbye to her now. Love Bert XXX.' His charge is an Austin K2 model, registered by Poole Town Council on 18 September 1942. It was allocated the Dorset mark ATK 742.

A Leyland Royal Flying Corps truck, pictured somewhere in Hampshire, 1916. Registered by the Secretary of State for War, at the War Office in London, this particular military vehicle was assigned the Hampshire mark AA 5789. It is rather unfortunate that just a few years ago some short-sighted civil servant authorized the destruction of records relating to a number of Hampshire-registered motor vehicles from this period, so we are unable to reveal any details about the individual machine. The story of the Leyland RAF type is almost legendary. The company bought back more than 4000 war worn vehicles at the end of the First World War and set up a factory to recondition them for sale into the civilian market. Very many of the trucks were snapped up by budding transport operators and they gave years of excellent service, only later to be scrapped through obsolescence, rather than wear.

Following page, bottom: A photo opportunity for a Vulcan at Aldershot, 1929. This 6x4 30cwt cargo truck was one of several types manufactured for the War Office by Tilling-Stevens Motors Limited of Maidstone, Kent. Powered by a four-cylinder petrol engine, the model was designated the RSW. It had an unusual front spring arrangement, as seen in the photograph. With a set of overall tracks fitted to the rear wheels, the vehicle gave a very creditable performance over rough terrain. The Hampshire mark OU 3978 was released in December 1929.

A 'Dragon' taking a short-cut through a Wessex cornfield, in 1928. Here we can see a 30cwt Crossley semi-tracked Field Artillery Tractor towing an 18-pounder field gun and limber, near Perham Down, on the edge of Salisbury Plain. The half-track mechanism had been developed in France by the Kégresse company, which enjoyed a long association with Crossley Motors Limited, of Gorton, Manchester. Their first half-track was assembled in 1924. The gun crew shown here were representatives of 9th Field Brigade, Royal Artillery, who were taking part in a mechanized warfare exercise.

Army driver training in Dorset, in the early thirties. The six-wheeled cargo trucks shown here are believed to be derivatives of the D-series model, produced by Morris Commercial in Birmingham from 1927-1933. Powered by a four-cylinder petrol engine, the vehicle was designed to carry 30cwt on the road and 20cwt across country. With 4x2 drive they had a reasonably good cross-country performance.

Seven
The Power of Steam

Tasker's 'Hero', exhibited at the Southampton show in 1869. Hero was manufactured by Tasker and Sons at the Waterloo Iron Works, Upper Clatford, near Andover. Specified as a two-cylinder, 18hp, self-propelled engine, it was given works No.54. In the early 1880s, the machine was employed by the Electrical Insulator Manufacturing Company at the Rockingham Clay Works, West Wellow, which was at that time in the County of Wiltshire. A story survives about a young man named Herbert Smallbone who was employed to walk in front of the engine waving a red flag to warn others of its approach. He recalled on several occasions walking all the way to Collinbourne, Hungerford and Wilton from his base at Wellow. The original picture carries the imprint of J. Gaulton, photographer, of West Wellow.

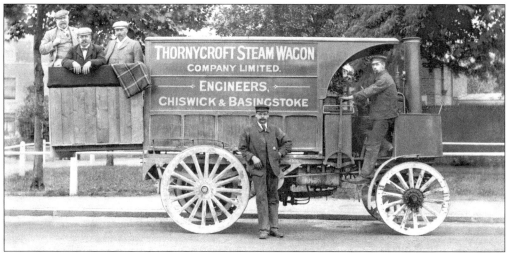

A Thornycroft steam lorry, manufactured in 1899. We have no idea why this particular photograph was taken. Perhaps it is a publicity picture associated with the move of equipment and personnel from the company's works in Chiswick to Basingstoke. We can see that this early Thornycroft two-ton steam wagon is running on wooden wheels fitted with iron bands. Later models had cast metal wheels.

Heather's Little Giant about to set off for Bournemouth in 1905. Here we can see a brown-coloured Tasker and Sons 'Little Giant' road locomotive about to depart from Waterloo Iron Works to be delivered to its new owner: Edward John Heather of 'The Hawthorns' Richmond Wood, Bournemouth. The machine was allocated the registration mark EL 302 on 27 July 1905. Eight years later, on 8 January 1913, Mr Heather sold the machine to Curtis and Sons of 180 Holdenhurst Road, Bournemouth. The engine continued working until December 1930, at which time the registration mark was cancelled.

A Hindley steam trolley manufactured in Bourton, Dorset in 1907. Messrs E.S. Hindley and Sons supplied this three-ton steam wagon to Jesse Long (fruit grower, jam maker and mineral water manufacturer) of Whitchurch, in April 1907. It carried the Hampshire mark AA 2184. The boiler of the vehicle was the subject of a patent, and it was known as 'Hindley's Stayless Locomotive' type, introduced in 1904. After only five or six years use, Jesse Long replaced the Hindley steamer with a petrol-engined, chain-driven, Scout van, made in Salisbury.

From Devon to Dorset in 1910. Here we can see the 'Greyhound' steam road locomotive (No.28258) that was displayed on the Richard Garrett and Sons' trade stand at the Devon show. It is understood that the machine was sold, while still on display, to Stephen and Arthur Moore (farmers and hay dealers) of Thornford, Dorset. When this photograph was taken the machine was working for George Smart and Sons (coal, coke and salt factors) of 10 Oakfield Street, Blandford. It carried the East Suffolk registration mark BJ 889.

The Speedwell pantechnicon in Southampton, 12 March 1913. Frederick William Smith purchased this 'Little Giant' steam wagon from W. Tasker and Sons Limited in October 1912. A standard five-ton wagon (No.1517), with screw jack and pump lubricator, complete with a 13' 6" body and hauling chain, it cost Mr Smith £483 17s 6d, as well as a £1 registration fee for the Hampshire mark AA 5047. A number of additional fittings and pieces of equipment were supplied: bottom boards to run long-ways on the platform, coal bunker at the back, three rings on each side of the body, one pair of piano steps, thirty feet of suction hose, a spring draw-bar, lamps, tools and the usual maintenance outfit. The vehicle was sign-written on the bunkers and along the side of the platform. A brass nameplate lettered 'Speedwell' was attached to the front of the engine. Easy payment terms were agreed: £100 with order, £100 on delivery and the balance to be completed by April 1913.

Following page, bottom: A Garrett three-way tipping wagon for Miles of Charminster, 1930. Registered with the Dorset mark TK 4100 on 22 March 1930, this sturdy steam wagon was allocated Garrett's works No.35376. Kenneth Miles was a sand and gravel haulage contractor who worked quite often for Dorset County Council. The firm was still very active until the late 1960s.

An Aveling and Porter rolling the roads of Wiltshire, 1921. This ten-ton single-cylinder steamroller (No.6676) is just one of a fleet of thirty machines supplied to the Wiltshire Steamroller Company by Aveling and Porter Limited of Rochester, Kent. The proprietors were Barnes Brothers of Southwick, Wiltshire. The thirty machines were allocated a batch of Wiltshire registration marks: HR 4385 to HR 4414 in April 1921.

Acknowledgements

It seems unbelievable to me now that it was nearly twenty years ago when I first thought about producing a book of local road transport. The time has passed by so very quickly, yet I have seen, learnt and experienced so much in that time. It has been a great pleasure to meet the hundreds of people with whom I have come into contract during the course of my collecting and research and many of them I now consider friends.

A number of individuals who have similar interests to my own have generously given help and advice whenever it was needed. They all posses superb photograph, postcard and/or motoring memorabilia collections to which I have been given access, when my own library was lacking. One meets certain people only once or twice in a lifetime, but the following names crop up time and time again, although it is far too long since I last enjoyed the company of one or two of them. They are Norman Aish, Nick Baldwin, David Fitton, Bryan K. Goodman, David Hales, Tim Harding, Peter Parrish, Eric Parsons, Phil Sposito, S.W. Stevens-Stratten and Mike Worthington-Williams. I am grateful to each and every one for all the help and encouragement over the years. My book would have been much the poorer had it not been for their involvement.

The success of a photographic collection such as this depends very much on the contributions of others. I would like to say a big thank you to the following individuals and organizations who have helped in so many different ways: Bill Body, Tony Bollen, H.W. Boulter, Wendy M.A. Bowen (Historic Photographic Collections Officer, Hampshire Museum Service), Nigel Bown, Jean Cox, Peter Crocker, Mrs M. Cruse, Bill Dawe, the staff at Dorset County Archive Service, Dorset Police, Peter Drake, Harry Edwards (Club Historian, Morris Register), Malcolm Grace, L.G. Graham, Mrs Joyce Gowman, Robert Grieves, Sylvia Hale, the staff at Hampshire County Record Office, Barbara Hillier, Robert H Johnson, Neale Lawson, John Manley, Robert 'Bob' Moorman, Derrick Mould, the Archivists at the National Motor Museum Library, Mrs Jeremy Nieboer, Mike Pettigrew, Roger Pope, the staff at Salisbury Local Studies Library, the staff at Southampton City Record Office, Phillipa Stevens (Local Studies Librarian at Winchester), Richard Stower, Betty and Dave Underwood (Classic Pictures, of Christchurch), William Webb, Harry Withers and Steve Woodward.

Finally, I must acknowledge the considerable contribution made by the managers and staff at the Wiltshire County Record Office in Trowbridge. I have benefited from their services on hundreds of occasions during the past twenty years or so and on each and every visit I have received nothing but enthusiasm and encouragement. If there were awards given out for the Best Record Office, they would surely have to be nominated. Thank you all very much indeed.

Peter R Daniels
Netherhampton
May 2000.